The Meaning of YOUR Life:

Build a Life That Matters—At Any Age, Any Stage

Copyright Page

The Meaning of YOUR Life:
Build a Life That Matters—At Any Age, Any Stage
© 2025 Ken Konet, M.Ed., MBA, & Ibrahim Roble
All rights reserved.

For information, contact:
Ken Konet & Ibrahim Roble
Humbolton Press, LLC
Dallas, Texas

ISBN (Paperback): [ISBN: 978-1-966703-11-2]
ISBN (Kindle): [ISBN: 978-1-966703-12-9]

First Edition – 2025

Printed in the United States of America.

Cover design and artwork by Ken Konet
Interior layout by Ken Konet

Disclaimer

This book is intended for informational and inspirational purposes only. It is not a substitute for professional mental health, medical, or legal advice. The authors and publisher disclaim any liability arising directly or indirectly from the use or application of the contents of this book.

Credits and Acknowledgments

The authors wish to thank the readers, learners, and seekers of all ages who continue to ask better questions about life, purpose, and meaning.

Table of Contents

Copyright Page.................................2

How to Use This Book 6

Introduction: 8

Chapter 1: Survival & Continuity 13

Chapter 2: Consciousness & Awareness 25

Chapter 3: Connection & Belonging.......38

Chapter 4: Growth & Learning – Leveling Up IRL 50

Chapter 5: Purpose & Contribution – Why Do You Matter?.............................61

Chapter 6: Joy & Experience 72

Chapter 7: Suffering & Transcendence – The Pain That Shapes Us...........................82

Chapter 8: Ethics & Responsibility – How to Live Without Being a Jerk 93

Chapter 9: Spiritual & Cosmic Context – Plugging Into Something Bigger............107

Chapter 10: Mortality & Legacy – The Final Exam 118

Chapter 11: So What Now? – Living the Meaning Day by Day 129

Chapter 12 : Conclusion...........................136

Epilogue 142

How to Use This Book
(Or, How Not to Get Lost in It)

You're holding a field guide, not a sermon.
This isn't a book you read once and shelf is one
you live with, argue with, laugh at, and return to
when life decides to throw another plot twist
your way.

Here's the deal: The Meaning of YOUR Life was
built for *you*, at whatever stage you happen to be
in right now—twelve or ninety-nine, thriving or
just surviving. Each chapter tackles one of the
ten foundations of meaning—survival, awareness,
connection, growth, purpose, joy, suffering,
ethics, wonder, and legacy—and within each,
you'll find reflections, lessons, and small
experiments for every age group.

You don't need to read it in order. You can skip
to the chapter you need today. Maybe you're
twenty and lost. Maybe you're fifty and
exhausted. Maybe you're eighty and wondering
what it all added up to. Pick your chapter. It'll
still make sense. Life isn't linear; this book isn't
either.

At the end of every chapter, you'll see a section
called "Actions." Think of these as reality
anchors—simple practices that make the

philosophy stick. You're not expected to do them all. Choose one. Try it. Fail at it. Try again. Meaning builds through repetition, not perfection.

You'll also see age lenses throughout the book:

- **12-Year-Old Explorer** — the beginner's curiosity and courage

- **18–29 Adventurer** — the experimenter's chaos and resilience

- **30–60 Chaos Survivor** — the grinder's wisdom and balance

- **60–99 Legacy Keeper** — the mentor's peace and reflection

Those are not boxes; they're mirrors. You'll recognize pieces of yourself in more than one. That's the point. We grow in loops, not lines.

So read slowly. Write in the margins. Dog-ear the pages that hit too close.
And if at any point you think, *"I wish someone had told me this years ago,"*—well, that's your cue to pass the book to someone younger. That's how meaning multiplies.

Ready? Good! Let's begin with the simplest truth there is—you're here. You exist. And that's already a miracle worth understanding.

Introduction:

Congratulations, You Exist. Now What?

Congratulations, traveler. Against cosmic odds, you've been plopped into existence. You didn't click "I agree," you didn't sign a waiver, and you definitely didn't get a tutorial level explaining the rules. One minute: *nonexistence.* The next minute: *boom— taxes, TikTok, and the terrifying awareness that you have to figure out what the hell life means.*

For the 12-Year-Old (Curious Explorer)

Imagine life like a video game where you didn't get to pick your character—hair, stats, parents, all preloaded. You're stuck with "default skin," kiddo. But here's the cheat code: every side quest you try (friendships, hobbies, even embarrassing TikTok dances) adds XP. Your only job right now? Play. Explore. Screw up. Laugh. Learn. The main quest will reveal itself as you go.

For the 18–29-Year-Old (Early Adult Adventurer)

Welcome to the *"I'm an adult, I think?"* stage. You've got freedom, responsibilities, and a constant fear you're wasting your twenties. You eat cereal at midnight, panic about rent, wonder if your degree was a scam, and doomscroll your friends' fake-perfect lives on Instagram.

Meaning, for you, is less about "finding your purpose" and more about building one brick at a time—through messy relationships, trial-and-error jobs, heartbreaks, side hustles, and epic karaoke nights that you'll only half-remember. This is your sandbox decade. Mistakes aren't failures—they're beta tests.

For the 30–60-Year-Old (Chaos Survivor)

Ah, adulthood proper: the stage where life feels like juggling flaming swords while riding a unicycle on a tightrope above a pit of alligators. You've got bills, deadlines, kids (human or furry), aging parents, a boss that might be an algorithm, and an attention span shredded by constant notifications.

Meaning here isn't found in grand philosophies—it's in survival hacks. It's in the tiny pockets of peace you carve out between meetings. It's in choosing presence over burnout, kindness over cynicism, laughter over despair. You're not just asking, *"Why am I here?"* You're asking, *"How do I keep this circus from burning down?"*

For the 60–99-Year-Old (Legacy Keeper)

And finally, the twilight years. The stage where you've played most of the levels, collected most of the loot, and now you're asking the Big Final Boss question: *Did my life matter?* Fear is real here—fear of endings, of being forgotten, of time running out.

But here's the balm: meaning isn't measured in trophies or titles. It's measured in love given, laughter shared, kindness passed on. You've already left fingerprints on hearts, echoes in stories, ripples in the people you've touched. Legacy isn't built in stone; it lives in the lives you shaped.

The Common Thread

Different ages, different anxieties. But the question is always the same: *What's the point of all this?* Philosophers gave us answers: Plato said virtue, Nietzsche said power, Buddhists said peace, capitalism says "buy more stuff." Grandma says "eat your vegetables."

The truth? There's no single magic answer. The question is timeless. What changes is the **context**.

- Socrates never had to update his iPhone.

- Buddha never got spam calls about his camel's extended warranty.

- Marcus Aurelius never dealt with middle management or TikTok.

- Jesus never had to explain NFTs.

But *you* do. You're alive in the **Dumpster Fire Era™**: climate anxiety, social media comparison, AI writing your essays, and existential dread available on demand, 24/7.

The Ken & Ibrahim Promise

Here's what this book will—and will not—do.

X It will not hand you The Answer™. Anyone who claims they have it is probably trying to sell you a $499 online course.

✓ It will give you a map: the **Ten timeless foundations of meaning**—survival, awareness, connection, growth, purpose, joy, suffering, ethics, spirituality, and legacy—updated for modern chaos.

"We'll laugh, we'll roast ourselves, we'll face uncomfortable truths, and at the end of it you'll have a compass—not to find "The Meaning of Life," but to live your meaning every day. Think of us less as a guru on a mountaintop and more as that friend who shows up with a shovel at 3 a.m. to help you bury the evidence. No questions asked."

Why Keep Reading?

Because whether you're twelve and exploring, twenty-five and experimenting, forty and exhausted, or ninety-nine and reflecting, the same truth holds: **life's meaning isn't something you wait to discover, it's something you create.**

And here's the kicker: if you can learn to laugh at the void, it can't swallow you whole.

So, let's start.

Chapter 1: Survival & Continuity

A: Staying Alive in the Age of Chaos

Let's start where all the great questions about life should begin: with the most obvious and the most ignored truth. **You have to be alive for any of this to matter.** I know, I know—sounds like Captain Obvious showed up to your existential crisis. But think about it. Survival is the ground floor. No survival, no purpose. No survival, no TikTok. No survival, no awkward family holidays where everyone pretends the cranberry sauce matters more than the fact that Uncle Greg is on his fifth beer.

In the old days, survival was simple: don't get eaten by a lion, don't starve, don't drink swamp water. Congratulations, you lived another day. In our shiny modern era, the lions have been replaced with credit card debt, doomscrolling until 3 a.m., stress-induced migraines, and forgetting to drink water because you're "too busy." Same game, new bosses. Our ancestors wrestled saber-toothed tigers. We wrestle with the Wi-Fi router. Honestly, I'm not sure who has it worse."

Here's the kicker: you can't skip this level. No cheat code. Survival is the default meaning of existence. You're here, you're breathing, and your body is basically screaming at you every day: *Keep me running, damn it.* But here's the twist. It's not just about surviving. It's about **continuity**—keeping the chain going. Not only staying alive, but living in such a way that your existence adds something, even if that something is just being the one person in your friend group who knows how to restart the Wi-Fi.

And here's where it gets fun. Survival doesn't look the same at twelve as it does at twenty-five, or fifty, or ninety-nine. At twelve, survival is not breaking your wrist while trying parkour because you saw it on YouTube. At twenty-five, it's making sure your rent clears and you don't subsist entirely on gas station burritos. At fifty, it's keeping your sanity while everything in your calendar screams "urgent." At ninety-nine, survival looks like keeping your body humming long enough to share one more story with the grandkids.

This chapter is about zooming in on that foundation: **what it means to stay alive, at different stages of life, in the middle of a world that often feels like it's designed to kill your joy, your health, or your will to get out of bed.**

So let's talk about survival—not as a boring biology class, but as a universal quest. Your quest. My quest. The human quest. The one meaning every single one of us shares, whether you're a 12-year-old with a Fortnite addiction, a twenty-something juggling side hustles, a forty-something juggling mortgages and therapy, or a ninety-nine-year-old wondering if all those salads were worth it.

Because without survival, there's nothing. But with survival? There's everything else.

B: Survival for the 12-Year-Old Explorer

At twelve, survival feels like the easiest thing in the world because you've never really had to think about it. Someone else cooks the meals, pays the bills, and makes sure you don't forget a jacket when it's forty degrees out. You don't worry about health insurance, rent, or whether eating gas station sushi at midnight will end badly. Your job right now is simpler: *don't fall off your bike, don't eat things you found on the ground, and for the love of everything holy, don't microwave aluminum foil.*

But here's the thing: survival at twelve is more than just "don't die." It's the foundation of how you're going to treat survival for the rest of your life. Right now, you're programming your brain, wiring your habits. If you live off energy drinks and spicy chips, your body will politely tolerate it... for now. But your future self is watching, arms crossed, waiting to yell at you for being an idiot.

Think of your body like a video game character. You've been assigned this avatar, and it comes with health stats, stamina, and energy bars. You don't get to trade it in for a new one later, so you'd better take care of the one you've got. Eat decent food, sleep sometimes, and for the love of your XP bar, move around. Survival is just basic maintenance of your character—keeping them from glitching out before you get to the good quests.

But survival at twelve also means learning resilience. You're going to get teased, you're going to fail at something (a test, a sport, a crush), and you're going to feel like it's the end of the world. Spoiler: it's not. Those little failures are practice runs. They're how you build the survival muscles you'll need later when the stakes get higher. Every time you fall, every time you get embarrassed, every time you screw something up and keep going—that's survival.

And here's the twist: survival at twelve isn't supposed to feel like a lecture. It's supposed to feel like play. You survive by exploring, by trying new things, by laughing at yourself when you mess up. Life right now isn't about winning; it's about *loading the map.* The better you get at exploring without fear, the stronger your survival game will be when the monsters get bigger later.

So yeah, survival at twelve isn't about dodging lions or paying rent. It's about learning how to play the game without rage-quitting.

C: Survival for the 18–29 Adventurer

Here it is: the era you thought you were waiting for. You're finally an adult. No one can tell you when to go to bed, what to eat, or whether you're allowed to watch that R-rated movie. You are free. Which sounds fantastic until you realize freedom comes with a thousand new ways to screw up survival.

Suddenly, no one is packing your lunches. You're buying groceries, and somehow half of them are frozen pizza rolls. You're paying rent—sometimes late, sometimes with the precision of a bomb defusal. You're managing work, school, maybe relationships, maybe debt, maybe all of the above, and meanwhile, you're also supposed to be building a future. Survival feels less like "don't get eaten by a lion" and more like "don't drown under the crushing weight of your own to-do list."

At this stage, survival often gets confused with success. You think surviving means *crushing it*: having the perfect job, the perfect apartment, the perfect love life, and an Instagram feed that makes your friends jealous. But here's the truth: survival in your twenties isn't about crushing it. It's about not being crushed.

That means failing without deciding you're a failure. Getting rejected from jobs and remembering that rejection is a step, not a death sentence. Breaking up with someone and realizing it doesn't mean you're unlovable—it means you dodged a bad main quest. Losing money, missing opportunities, making mistakes, and still waking up the next day ready to try again. That's survival in this decade.

You're building your foundation brick by shaky brick. Some bricks will crack. Some will crumble. That's fine. Your survival is about resilience—about not giving up when the tower wobbles. You don't need to have all the answers yet. You don't even need to have most of them. You just need to stay in the game.

And here's the kicker: survival in your twenties comes with temptation. You'll want shortcuts.

17

Instant gratification. You'll want to skip to the "I figured out my purpose" chapter. But if you skip the mess, you skip the growth. The chaos is part of the continuity.

So survival here isn't glamorous. It's ramen nights and side hustles, breakups and breakthroughs, rent payments and road trips. It's learning to live with uncertainty without letting it swallow you.

You don't have to thrive yet. You just have to keep going.

D: Survival for the 30–60 Chaos Survivor

Welcome to the main event. The "middle years." The era of flaming-sword juggling. Survival here isn't a backdrop anymore—it's the whole show. You are running a marathon while also carrying a backpack filled with bricks labeled "responsibilities."

You're juggling jobs, families, bills, and maybe the dog who keeps eating the couch. You're not just keeping *yourself* alive—you're keeping whole systems alive. Kids who expect meals. Bosses who expect deadlines. Aging parents who suddenly need your help. And let's not even talk about how your body is betraying you with mysterious creaks, aches, and a metabolism that just gave up on your side of the deal.

Survival here is less about raw energy and more about strategy. At this point, you can't simply power through on adrenaline and optimism. You have to choose carefully. What you eat, how much you sleep, who you spend time with—it all matters. You

18

don't bounce back the way you did at twenty-five, which means surviving requires actual intentionality.

And survival here isn't just physical. It's mental. It's emotional. It's trying to avoid burnout when your calendar looks like it was designed by a sadistic game developer. It's learning to say no without guilt. It's realizing that the constant grind doesn't actually lead to happiness, it just leads to you googling "symptoms of stress-induced ulcers" at 2 a.m.

Here's the dirty little secret: survival at this stage isn't heroic. It's boring. It's keeping the machine running. Paying the mortgage. Showing up to work. Getting your kids to school on time. Checking in on your parents. Folding laundry. Again. And again. And again. Continuity becomes the name of the game—because you are the glue holding a whole web of lives together.

But within the monotony, there's meaning. Survival here isn't about drama—it's about endurance. The small acts, the daily grind, the fact that you keep showing up even when you're exhausted—that's your victory. You're not slaying dragons. You're surviving the endless little cuts of stress, and somehow, in the middle of it all, you're keeping the circus from collapsing.

It might not feel glamorous, but this is where survival becomes sacred. Because without you, so many other lives would fall apart.

E: Survival for the 60–99 Legacy Keeper

19

By the time you've crossed into the later decades, survival has morphed again. It's no longer about proving yourself or holding everything together for everyone else. Now survival feels like an act of both rebellion and grace. Every morning you wake up, stretch, and realize, *Hey, I'm still here,* you've already won the first battle of the day.

At this stage, survival isn't about building a foundation or carrying others on your back. It's about tending the fire you've kept alive for so long. The questions shift. Not "How do I pay rent?" or "How do I juggle kids and work?" but "How much time do I have, and how do I spend it in a way that feels like living, not just waiting?"

And here's the part no one wants to say out loud: survival gets scary here. Every ache feels louder. Every medical appointment comes with background anxiety. Friends start disappearing. Mortality stops being an abstract philosophical concept and starts being a guest who never leaves the party. It can feel terrifying.

But survival now is less about defying death and more about cherishing life. Every laugh with a grandchild, every story told around a table, every sunset you actually take the time to notice—those are victories. Continuity here isn't about building new empires. It's about passing on the torch. Your stories, your wisdom, your love—that's what continues.

And survival doesn't mean pretending you're not afraid. It means acknowledging the fear and living anyway. It means telling the truth about your life, even the messy parts, so others can learn from it. It means letting go of things you can't control and holding tight to the moments that still spark joy.

If you've made it this far, you've already proven yourself. You've survived every decade's version of chaos, and now survival is less about endurance and more about savoring. Less about continuity of your body, more about continuity of your spirit in the people and places you've touched.

So yes, survival here is fragile. But it's also radiant. Every day is borrowed time—and that makes each one infinitely precious.

F: Ken Commentary – Survival Isn't Sexy, But It's Sacred

Here's the truth no one wants to put on a motivational poster: survival is boring. It's not climbing Everest or slaying dragons. It's brushing your teeth, paying your bills, making sure you drink water before you pass out, and keeping your blood pressure low enough that your doctor doesn't glare at you. Survival is the unglamorous grind, the background noise of being alive.

And yet—without it, nothing else matters. No growth, no joy, no purpose, no legacy. You don't get to skip this part of the syllabus. You survive first, then you do literally everything else.

The funny part is how survival shapeshifts across the decades. At twelve, it's about not licking electrical outlets and building the early habits that will either save or ruin you later. At twenty-five, it's about tripping, failing, panicking, and still waking up the next day to try again. At forty-five, it's about managing the circus without burning down the tent. At ninety-nine, it's about savoring every day that your body lets you stick around.

Different stages, same theme: survival isn't glamorous, but it's your baseline victory.

And here's the kicker: in a world like ours—chaotic, noisy, AI writing half the internet, climate disasters on the news every other Tuesday—basic survival is harder than it looks. Not physical survival, necessarily, but mental survival. Emotional survival. Soul survival. The ability to get through the day without deciding it's all meaningless.

This is where continuity enters the picture. It's not just "I made it to Thursday." It's "I made it to Thursday and carried something forward." Maybe you raised a kid. Maybe you kept a friendship alive. Maybe you wrote a poem, planted a tree, or just refused to let cynicism win. Survival plus continuity is what gives life momentum.

Of course, survival doesn't get headlines because it doesn't feel dramatic. Nobody writes ballads about flossing or getting seven hours of sleep. But in reality, those small, repetitive, unsexy acts are the real foundation of everything meaningful. Without them, the shiny stuff crumbles.

So let us say it clearly: if you've made it this far, if you're still here—congratulations. You've already nailed the first meaning of life. You survived. And now we get to talk about what comes next.

G: Actions – Practicing Survival & Continuity

For the 12-Year-Old Explorer

Try treating your body like a game character for one week. Drink water, get sleep, eat at least one actual vegetable. Track it like XP. Every good habit adds points. Every skipped one lowers your stamina bar. See how much stronger your "player" feels by the end of the week.

For the 18–29 Adventurer

Pick one thing you've been procrastinating out of fear—sending the application, having the conversation, taking the risk—and just do it. Don't wait until you "feel ready." Survival in your twenties is about stacking attempts, not waiting for perfection. Your future self won't remember the awkwardness; they'll remember you tried.

For the 30–60 Chaos Survivor

Audit your calendar. Circle one thing that is draining you but doesn't actually matter, then cut it. Survival here is not about doing more; it's about preserving your sanity by doing less of the pointless. Protect your energy like it's a limited resource—because it is.

For the 60–99 Legacy Keeper

Plant a tree that will grow long after you're gone, or write down a family recipe and cook it with someone younger. Legacy isn't just in stories told; it's in life that continues.

And with that, **Chapter 1: Survival & Continuity** is complete.

Chapter 2: Consciousness & Awareness

A: Opening Scene; Being Present While Doomscrolling

Congratulations again. You've survived the first chapter, which means you're still breathing, and that's excellent. But now comes the sequel, and like most sequels, it's trickier: **you have to actually notice that you exist.**

Survival is basic. Awareness is bonus content. Without awareness, you're basically a Roomba—bumping around, doing tasks, occasionally stuck in a corner, but never really understanding the room you're in. With awareness, you become... well, still a little messy, but at least you *know* you're messy.

The great philosophers all knew this. The problem? They didn't have to do it in a world where your phone pings every ten seconds, Netflix asks "Are you still watching?" like a passive-aggressive roommate, and entire billion-dollar industries exist just to steal your attention. Marcus Aurelius could meditate on the meaning of life because nobody was sliding into his DMs at 2 a.m.

And that's why awareness today is more important than ever. You can survive without it—you can wake up, go to work, pay bills, eat dinner, go back to bed, repeat—but you'll be living on autopilot. Days blur into weeks, weeks blur into years, and one morning you wake up at thirty-five wondering why life feels like one long loading screen.

Awareness breaks the loop. It's the pause button that lets you step back and say, *Oh right, I'm alive, and this moment is happening now.* It's not mystical; it's practical. Awareness lets you actually taste the coffee instead of inhaling it while checking emails. It lets you hear the laugh of someone you love instead of scrolling while they talk. It lets you look at a sunset without feeling the urge to post it before you've even looked at it.

And here's the kicker: in the age of chaos and code, awareness isn't a luxury. It's survival's sequel. Because what's the point of surviving if you never notice you're alive?

You're Not a Roomba

So, survival you've got down—congratulations, you're still breathing. But existing without awareness is like winning a lifetime supply of pizza and never taking the time to actually taste a slice. Survival keeps you alive. Awareness reminds you that life is happening while you're busy doomscrolling headlines about how everything is on fire.

Let us put it this way: without awareness, you're basically a Roomba. You wake up, bounce around, avoid obstacles (sometimes), bump into the same corner twelve times, make a little noise, and eventually dock at the charger until tomorrow. No reflection, no savoring, no "holy crap, I'm alive." Just… beeping around until the battery dies. The only difference is that the Roomba doesn't occasionally stop mid-clean, stares into the void, and wonder if it should have become a blender instead.

Awareness is the pause button on autopilot. It's the split-second when you notice your coffee isn't just hot brown liquid but actually has a flavor. It's catching the ridiculous, full-throated snort-laugh your best friend makes when they think no one's listening. It's looking at a sunset and remembering that your own eyes have a higher resolution than your phone's camera, anyway.

Of course, awareness today is harder than it's ever been. We live in the distraction Olympics. Everything is designed to hijack your attention: your phone pings, your apps scream, YouTube autoplays a video about building a log cabin, and suddenly it's 3 a.m. and you're checking Zillow for plots of land in Alaska, and even refrigerators are getting smart enough to tell you you're out of milk and dignity. It's not just lions and famine anymore—it's notifications. The modern predator isn't a beast with claws; it's a dopamine slot machine in your pocket.

The trap is that a life without awareness is still, technically, a life. You can punch the clock, pay the bills, clear your inbox, and inhale a sandwich while scrolling through videos of other people's dogs. You can go to bed, repeat, and keep your vital signs humming along just fine. But that's not living. That's being a background character in your own movie—you're on screen, but you're not driving the plot.

Awareness cracks the blur open. It's how you notice moments before they dissolve into the background. It's what makes an ordinary Tuesday lunch something you'll remember twenty years later. It's the difference between "I ate" and "I savored."

So here's the mission for this chapter: wake up. Learn to notice. Learn to stop living like a Roomba on shuffle mode and start paying attention to the fact that you're actually here, right now, in this weird, stressful, meme-filled, miraculous world.

B: Awareness for the 12-Year-Old Explorer

At twelve, you don't think about awareness because the world is basically one giant "ooh, shiny!" machine. Every day is full of new discoveries, distractions, and questions that start with "why." Why is the sky blue? Why do dogs sniff each other's butts? Why do adults look so tired all the time? Curiosity is baked into you at this age, which is why awareness is both natural and fragile here.

Here's what happens: adults start teaching you to tune out. "Stop daydreaming." "Focus on the worksheet." "Pay attention" usually means "ignore your own curiosity and do what I'm telling you." The tragedy? You actually *are* paying attention, you're just paying attention to the wrong thing, at least by adult standards.

But awareness at twelve isn't about shutting curiosity down. It's about noticing more deeply. It's realizing that the tree you walk past every day changes colors with the seasons, or that your best friend laughs in three different ways depending on the joke, or that silence sometimes has a sound. It's learning to pay attention on purpose, not just when something explodes in front of you.

Awareness for you right now is a kind of superpower. You see things adults miss. You notice details because your brain hasn't been trained to filter everything out. That's not a bug—it's a feature. The danger is that if you don't practice it, you'll lose it. You'll end up like the grown-ups who scroll through their phones while walking into traffic.

So here's the challenge: keep noticing. Keep wondering. Awareness is more than just being awake; it's being awake to *this moment,* to the weirdness and beauty happening around you right now. If you can hold onto that skill as you grow, you'll be light-years ahead of the rest of us who forgot how.

C: Awareness for the 18–29 Adventurer

Here's the thing about your twenties: you think you're supposed to have it all figured out, and the universe laughs at you every time you try. You're testing careers, relationships, identities, cities, maybe even hairstyles that will haunt your Facebook photos forever. On the outside, it looks like you're hustling, experimenting, chasing freedom. On the inside, you're often running on autopilot, bouncing between stress, comparison, and the vague hope that someone, somewhere, will hand you the map you misplaced.

Awareness at this stage isn't just about noticing sunsets or savoring your latte foam—it's about noticing *yourself.* It's realizing you're not just a hamster on a wheel. You're a human being with feelings, patterns, and blind spots. And those blind spots are sneaky. One day you wake up and realize you've been numbing yourself with work, or alcohol, or binge-watching shows until 3 a.m., and you can't even remember why you started.

Awareness here is the first step toward breaking the cycle. It's asking: *Why am I doing this? Do I even like this? Is this mine, or am I just copying someone else's idea of success?* It's pausing before you say yes to the relationship, the job, the move, and asking if it aligns with who you actually are—or who you're pretending to be.

This is where awareness gets uncomfortable, because it doesn't let you hide. It shines a flashlight on your habits, your insecurities, your desperate attempts to look like you have it together. But here's the good news: awareness is not judgment. It's not about shaming yourself for mistakes; it's about catching them in real time so you can pivot.

Without awareness, your twenties can become one long autopilot loop of chasing approval, scrolling envy, and numbing out. With awareness, you start building actual agency. You stop reacting to life and start shaping it. You realize that maybe it's okay not to have it all figured out—as long as you're awake enough to notice what's happening while you figure it out.

Survival got you into your twenties. Awareness is what will keep you from sleepwalking through them.

D: Awareness for the 30–60 Chaos Survivor

By the time you hit your thirties, forties, fifties, survival isn't the question anymore—it's how to keep your sanity while you juggle more spinning plates than a circus performer hopped up on espresso. You've got bills, jobs, kids (or pets you treat like kids), aging parents, marriages, divorces, maybe remarriages, and a calendar that looks like a cruel joke written in Outlook.

This is where awareness turns from nice-to-have into absolutely necessary. Because without awareness, these years blur together into one long grind. You wake up, rush, work, stress, eat standing up, collapse, repeat. Blink once and you're 38. Blink again and suddenly you're 52, wondering where the last decade went and why your back makes that noise.

Awareness here isn't some mystical retreat on a mountaintop. It's as simple and as hard as noticing what's happening while it's happening. It's realizing when you're snapping at your partner not because they deserve it, but because you haven't slept properly in weeks. It's catching yourself answering emails at midnight and asking, *Is this actually important, or am I just addicted to the grind?* It's hearing your kid's story about their day and actually listening instead of nodding while scrolling Twitter.

The irony is that in this stage, you know more about life than you ever did before—but you have less time to notice any of it. The stress eats your attention. The noise drowns out the meaning. Without awareness, you're not living these years, you're enduring them. With awareness, you start to reclaim them piece by piece.

That doesn't mean burning sage and chanting in a linen robe. It means micro-moments. A deep breath before a meeting. A pause before you say yes to something you'll regret. A choice to sit down for dinner without your phone. Tiny cracks in the autopilot wall.

Because here's the truth: awareness in these years is the difference between life feeling like a blur of responsibility and life feeling like a story you're actually inside of. And the more you practice, the more you start to notice—hey, even in the chaos, there are pockets of beauty worth remembering.

E: Awareness for the 60–99 Legacy Keeper

By the time you reach the later decades, awareness stops being a buzzword and becomes a lifeline. It's no longer about optimizing productivity or finding your career path—it's about savoring. Every moment is sharper because you know there are fewer of them left. The stakes are different now.

Survival is still part of the game, sure—doctor visits, prescriptions, moving a little slower than you'd like—but awareness is what turns those years from waiting into living. It's the difference between sitting in a chair and feeling like life has passed you by, versus noticing the light in the room, the laughter of family, the taste of one more cup of coffee. Awareness here is presence distilled to its purest form: *I'm still here, and this moment matters.*

At this stage, awareness is also memory's ally. The more present you are, the more stories you carry, and the more vividly you can pass them on. You've seen enough of life to know that time is slippery. Awareness helps you hold it a little tighter. When you tell your grandkids about your first love, or that time you hitchhiked across the country, or the hilarious disaster at your first job, awareness is what makes the memory alive again instead of just a faded headline.

And yes, there's fear in these years. The awareness of mortality is no longer abstract—it's sitting across the table, sipping tea with you. But here's the hidden gift: that very awareness makes each day glow brighter. The ordinary becomes sacred. A shared laugh, a walk in the sun, even the silence between words—they all matter more because you are awake enough to notice them.

You don't have to chase meaning anymore. You only have to notice it. And sometimes, that noticing is the greatest legacy you can give—reminding the rest of us who are rushing and distracted that life is here, now, not later.

F: Ibrahim Commentary – The Art of Noticing Before Life Blurs Out

Here's the thing about awareness: everyone talks about it like it's this magical Zen enlightenment moment where you float above the nonsense of life and suddenly become Buddha with Wi-Fi. Spoiler: it's not. Awareness is rarely majestic. Most of the time it's awkward, ordinary, and stupidly simple. It's the pause before you open another email. It's realizing you've been scrolling for twenty minutes and you can't remember a single post. It's remembering to actually taste the sandwich you just inhaled. That's awareness.

The problem is, nobody gets famous for this stuff. There's no award ceremony for "Most Mindfully Drank a Cup of Coffee." You don't get promoted because you noticed the sound of rain. And yet, those tiny moments are what make life feel like life. Without awareness, the whole thing becomes one long smear of Thursdays.

And let's be honest, we are terrible at awareness these days. We've engineered entire industries to make sure we never notice the present. Notifications, ads, infinite feeds, autoplay—all of them designed to keep us running like lab rats pressing the dopamine button. If you ever feel like your brain is Swiss cheese, congratulations, you're not broken. You're just living in a casino designed by Silicon Valley.

But across every age, awareness is the thing that pulls you back from autopilot. At twelve, it's curiosity before school beats it out of you. At twenty-five, it's catching yourself before you lose years to numbing habits and Instagram envy. At forty-five, it's the sanity check that keeps you from burning out completely. At ninety-five, it's the secret sauce that makes every small joy feel like a miracle.

The joke is that awareness sounds boring—"pay attention," "be present," "slow down"—but in reality it's one of the most rebellious things you can do in a world that's hell-bent on distracting you. Awareness is punk rock. Awareness is flipping off the algorithm. Awareness is saying: *I'm here, right now, and I'm going to notice this moment before it slips away.*

So, here's the truth bomb: life doesn't hand out extra credit for living on autopilot. You don't get to relive the parts you missed. If you want your life to matter, start noticing it.

G: Actions – Practicing Awareness in Daily Life

For the 12-Year-Old Explorer
Tomorrow, pick one thing you normally ignore and give it your full attention for two minutes. Watch how the clouds move. Notice how your dog reacts when you scratch its ear. Listen to the sound of your own footsteps. That's awareness: paying attention to the tiny miracles you usually speed past.

For the 18–29 Adventurer
Start a one-line daily journal. Nothing dramatic— just write down one thing you noticed about yourself or the world each day. Maybe it's "I was cranky because I skipped breakfast," or "The train smelled like burnt popcorn," or "I felt jealous scrolling

Instagram, then remembered half of it is fake." One line is enough to catch yourself in the act of living.

For the 30–60 Chaos Survivor
Set up a micro-pause ritual. Before you answer an email, take two breaths. Before you open your calendar, ask, "Do I really need to say yes to this?" Before bed, put your phone down for five minutes and just sit with yourself. Awareness doesn't need hours—it thrives in seconds.

For the 60–99 Legacy Keeper
Invite someone younger to share a simple, slow experience with you—like listening to a full album without talking or watching a sunset without a phone. Your legacy is also in the attention you teach others to pay to the world.

And with that, **Chapter 2: Consciousness & Awareness – Being Present While Doomscrolling** is complete.

Chapter 3: Connection & Belonging

Family, Friends, Memes, and Digital Tribes

A: Opening Scene – Why We're Pack Animals With Wi-Fi

Here's a brutal truth about humans: for all our speeches about independence, we're basically pack animals with better hair products and Wi-Fi. We like to think of ourselves as rugged individuals—lone wolves, self-starters, independent thinkers—but the reality is, wolves don't actually do well alone. And neither do we.

Strip away the Netflix subscription and the DoorDash deliveries and what you've got underneath is a species that panics if it feels left out. The caveman who wandered off from the tribe didn't become the first motivational speaker. He became sabretooth lunch. And that first tribe, the original survival pack? That was family. Belonging wasn't optional; it was survival. If your people didn't like you, you were toast. That wiring hasn't gone anywhere.

Fast-forward a few thousand years and we've swapped bonfires for group chats, hunting parties for office teams, and oral storytelling for memes. Our tribes look different, but the need is the same. We want to know we're seen. We want to know we

38

matter. We want to feel like someone's got our back when the saber-tooth—or its modern equivalent, late-stage capitalism—shows up.

The problem is, not all belonging is real. Some of it's counterfeit. You can rack up a thousand Instagram followers and still feel like nobody actually knows you. You can join a workplace "family" only to discover that "family" means "we'll work you until you collapse." Heck, you can sit at a holiday dinner surrounded by people who share your DNA and feel like a complete stranger. You can slide into a fandom or political tribe and realize you've traded individuality for slogans.

Belonging has always been a source of meaning. The twist in our modern chaos is that it's easier than ever to feel like you belong without actually belonging. A meme can make you laugh and feel connected for three seconds. A like on your post can give you a dopamine hit. But the second the screen goes dark, so does the illusion.

And that's why this chapter matters. Belonging isn't just about fitting in; it's about being known. Really known. It's about finding people who see your weirdness and say, "Yes, you're one of us." It's about the difference between a friend who knows your favorite pizza topping and a friend who shows up at the hospital without being asked.

We are wired to connect. Deny it, and life shrinks into loneliness. Embrace it, and life expands into meaning. So whether your tribe is your family, your friends, your coworkers, or the Discord server where you argue about Star Wars lore at 2 a.m., this chapter is about how connection saves us, and how to spot the difference between true belonging and cheap knockoffs.

B: Belonging for the 12-Year-Old Explorer

At twelve, belonging feels like life or death. Your first lessons happen at home. Family is your default tribe, the training ground where you learn the rules of connection. It's where you figure out if love is unconditional or if it comes with strings attached. A loving family is the home base you launch from every morning; a stressful one can feel like the first battle of the day before you've even had breakfast.

But socially? School is where it matters more than almost anything else. Who you sit with at lunch, which group you're invited into, whether you get picked for the game or left behind—these tiny details feel enormous because they are. They're your first taste of what it means to be accepted or rejected by a tribe you didn't get assigned at birth.

School is basically a giant petri dish for belonging experiments. Nerds, athletes, band kids, gamers, drama kids—it's all little tribes, each with their own rituals and rules. Some of those tribes will accept you as you are. Some will try to reshape you to fit. And some will exclude you completely, and it'll sting like hell. That's because your brain is wired to treat belonging like survival. When you're not included, your body actually reacts as if you're in danger. Loneliness isn't just sadness—it's stress chemistry firing off like alarms.

Here's the wild part: belonging doesn't mean being like everyone else. True belonging means you get to show up weird, awkward, and fully yourself—and you're still accepted. The kids who make fun of you for liking anime or drawing or coding aren't your tribe. The ones who laugh with you instead of at you? Those are your people.

Awareness is important here, too. Notice how you feel around certain groups. Do you feel lighter, happier, safe? That's real belonging. Do you feel anxious, small, like you're constantly auditioning for approval? That's fake belonging, and it'll drain you.

At twelve, you don't get to choose every tribe—you're stuck in classrooms, sports teams, **and families**—but you can start learning to spot the difference between fitting in and actually belonging. And the sooner you learn that difference, the easier every stage of life after this one becomes.

C: Belonging for the 18–29 Adventurer

If your teenage years were boot camp for belonging, your twenties are the battlefield. Suddenly, you're free to choose your tribes. No more homeroom assignments or cafeteria seating charts. This is also the decade you start renegotiating your role within your family—shifting from kid to adult peer, which can be awkward, liberating, or both at the same time. Now it's roommates, coworkers, college friends, clubs, fandoms, and relationships that range from soulmate-level intensity to "what was I thinking." Belonging here feels electrifying, because for the first time, you're building it yourself.

But freedom comes with traps. In this decade, belonging can blur into losing yourself. You want so badly to be part of something that you'll bend, compromise, or even erase pieces of yourself just to stay in the group. You join the workplace "family," but that family is more about squeezing overtime out of you than hugging you at Thanksgiving. You fall into friend groups where the bond is real one night and toxic the next. You might even create what people call a "chosen family"—friends who fill the roles your biological family couldn't or wouldn't. You chase likes, follows, and validation from people who don't even know your middle name.

And then there are relationships. In your twenties, connection can feel like the ultimate belonging—the person who sees you, loves you, makes the loneliness stop. But when that relationship breaks, it can feel like being exiled from the only tribe that mattered. That's why heartbreak in this era cuts so deep—it's not just the loss of a person, it's the loss of a belonging.

But here's the twist: belonging in your twenties isn't about finding *the* tribe that defines you forever. It's about experimenting. Testing. Trying groups, jobs, communities, and yes, relationships, and learning what actually feels like home. Some tribes will fail you. Some will drain you. But each failed belonging teaches you something about what you need in the next.

The secret here is noticing when a group makes you more yourself versus less. If you leave a hangout feeling lighter, more alive, more "you," that's belonging. If you leave feeling small, drained, or like you need to perform to fit in, that's a counterfeit tribe. And the sooner you learn to spot the difference, the sooner you can stop wasting time auditioning for a role you were never meant to play.

In your twenties, connection isn't perfect. But it's the training ground for finding your real people, the ones who will walk with you through the decades to come.

D: Belonging for the 30–60 Chaos Survivor

By the time you hit your thirties and beyond, belonging stops being about who you sit with at lunch or which party you're invited to on Saturday night. Instead, it becomes about who shows up when the hard stuff happens. The "fun tribe" of your twenties starts thinning out. Some friends move away, some fade, some vanish into the black hole of raising toddlers or climbing corporate ladders. Suddenly, your circle is smaller, but sharper.

Here's the thing: you're surrounded by people—coworkers, kids, partners, neighbors—but proximity isn't the same as belonging. You can sit in a meeting with ten colleagues, go to a kid's soccer game with a hundred parents, **or** live in a house full of family, and still feel profoundly alone. In this stage, you often become the anchor of your own family, the person everyone else tethers themselves to. Belonging isn't about being included; it's about being essential. It's knowing someone will still love you after you step on their LEGO barefoot at 3 a.m. Loneliness at this stage is sneaky, because it doesn't come from being physically isolated. It comes from feeling emotionally unseen.

And this is where belonging takes work. You don't just stumble into it anymore—you have to cultivate

43

it. You have to make the phone call, schedule the dinner, send the text, keep the connection alive. And sometimes, in the middle of chaos, that feels like one more chore on a never-ending list. But here's the irony: the thing that feels optional is the thing that keeps you human. Without it, stress calcifies. You start to feel like you're carrying the weight of the world alone.

Real belonging at this stage is often less dramatic than it was in your twenties. It's not an all-night road trip or a wild party. It's a friend who remembers your birthday without Facebook reminding them. It's a partner who can tell you're about to snap before you even realize it. It's a group where you can sigh out loud and everyone knows exactly what you mean.

And yes, some tribes will fall apart. Some friendships won't survive the distance, the stress, or the years. That loss can hurt as much as heartbreak. But the ones that endure—the ones that stick through the job losses, the divorces, the illnesses—those are the tribes that give these years meaning.

Belonging here isn't flashy. It's steady. It's the quiet comfort of knowing there are a few people who see you not as "parent," "boss," "employee," or "caretaker," but as you. And when everything else feels like chaos, that kind of belonging isn't just nice—it's sanity.

E: Belonging for the 60–99 Legacy Keeper

By the time you reach the later decades, belonging changes its shape once more. It's no longer about fitting into cliques or hustling to find your people in a sea of strangers. It becomes about being remembered, included, and valued when the noise of life starts to quiet down. Often, this means returning to the tribe you started with: family.

This is the stage where belonging can feel fragile. Your kids are grown, maybe raising kids of their own. Friends you once shared everything with are scattered, or gone. Technology has rewritten the language of connection so fast it can feel like you've been left behind. Group chats, streaming culture, Discord servers—these things don't always include you, and sometimes that stings. The world feels like it's moved on, and you're watching it race by.

But belonging here also has a deeper, richer flavor. It's not about being popular or plugged in. It's about the circles that remain—the family dinners, the neighbors who check in, the community that still knows your name. It's about seeing your own history in the faces of your children and grandchildren. It's about the stories you share and the love you give away. Belonging becomes less about proving yourself and more about weaving yourself into the fabric of memory.

Awareness sharpens in these years too. You notice the ache of loneliness more clearly, but you also notice the beauty of connection more sharply. A grandchild climbing onto your lap, a friend calling just to say hello, a hand held in silence—these moments shine because you understand how rare and fleeting they are.

And here's the quiet truth: belonging at this stage isn't only about being accepted—it's about passing something on. Your presence, your stories, your lessons, your love—that's how you create continuity. That's how you make sure you belong not just in the moment, but in the generations that follow.

When you're ninety, belonging doesn't mean being invited to every party. It means knowing that when you're gone, the people you loved will still feel you in the way they live, laugh, and tell stories. It means knowing your family carries a piece of you forward. And that's the most profound kind of belonging there is.

F: Ken Commentary – Pack Animals in Denial

Here's the thing about belonging, nobody wants to admit how badly they need it. We strut around like lone wolves, pretending we're fine all by ourselves, while quietly aching for a pack to howl with. The myth of independence is cute, but let's be honest humans are needy creatures. You can survive without belonging, sure, but you'll be miserable. And miserable people don't make good philosophers, lovers, or parents. They just make good case studies for psychologists.

Every stage of life tells the same story in a different accent. At twelve, belonging is the lunch table politics that feel like world wars. At twenty-five, it's the desperate scramble to find your people, even if you lose yourself in the process. At forty-five, it's the fight to keep friendships alive while work and family eat your calendar. At ninety, it's the prayer that someone remembers you enough to show up and listen. Same need, different costumes.

And let's talk about the messiest tribe of all: family. We're sold the idea that family is automatic belonging. Sometimes it is. But sometimes, family is where you learn the sting of not belonging first. Just because you share blood doesn't mean you share a soul. True belonging has to be earned with trust, respect, and love—and if your family doesn't offer that, you have every right to build your own pack elsewhere. Don't let anyone guilt you into a counterfeit connection just because you share a last name.

And oh boy, the modern world loves to mess with this wiring. We're living in a golden age of counterfeit belonging. Likes, follows, and retweets feel like connection until you realize no one would notice if you disappeared tomorrow. "Workplace families" insist you belong, as long as you meet your quota. Influencer tribes welcome you, but only if you buy the merch and parrot the hashtags. We mistake attention for affection, inclusion for intimacy, and networking for friendship. Then we wonder why we still feel lonely.

Real belonging is quieter, simpler, and less Instagrammable. It's the friend who shows up with soup when you're sick, not the one who comments a heart emoji on your selfie. It's the family member who listens without judging. It's the people who see your flaws and stay anyway. It's being known, not just being included.

Here's the kicker: belonging isn't optional. You can deny it all you want, but your brain is wired for it. Loneliness isn't just sad, it's lethal. Studies keep telling us it kills as effectively as smoking a pack a day, but somehow "Stop Being Lonely" hasn't made it onto the Surgeon General's warning labels yet.

So let's stop pretending we're above it. You're not a lone wolf. You're not an island. You're not even particularly original in your need for connection. You're a pack animal with Wi-Fi. And if you want your life to mean something, you'd better make damn sure your pack is real.

G: Actions – Practicing Belonging in Real Life

For the 12-Year-Old Explorer: Pick one friend, classmate, or sibling and tell them something you genuinely like about them. Or, do one small, helpful thing for a family member without being asked. Not as a joke, not sarcastically… but real words. Watch what happens. Belonging grows in the soil of being seen and appreciated, and you get to practice that skill right now.

For the 18–29 Adventurer: Take inventory of your tribes. Write down the groups you belong to— friends, work, online communities, hobbies—and ask yourself one question: do they make me feel more myself or less? Add a section for your family: What is my relationship with them now? What do I want it to be? Keep feeding the tribes that fuel you. Starve the ones that drain you. Your time and energy are limited; invest them in people who actually see you.

For the 30–60 Chaos Survivor: Schedule one act of deliberate connection this week. A phone call, a dinner, a coffee with someone who matters. It could be a screen-free family meal or a call to a parent just to listen. Put it in your calendar like it's a business meeting, because if you don't, life's chaos will eat the time for you. Belonging doesn't survive on autopilot—you have to maintain it like a fire that goes out if you stop tending it.

For the 60–99 Legacy Keeper: Choose a story of belonging from your life—a friendship that lasted, a community that held you, a love that shaped you— and share it with someone younger. Bonus points if it's a family story they've never heard before. Passing on those stories not only affirms your belonging, it gives the next generation a map for finding their own.

Chapter 4: Growth & Learning – Leveling Up IRL

A: Opening Scene – Life as an RPG With No Cheat Codes

Growth is not optional. Everything grows or it dies, and humans are no exception. But we're the only species that insists on making growth sound like an elective. "Self-improvement," we call it, as though learning to handle life isn't as essential as breathing. Trees don't stand around debating whether they should bother adding another ring. Cats don't hold off on hunting until they've read the latest productivity hack. Growth isn't a hobby. It's survival with better lighting.

The problem is, humans keep confusing growth with achievement. We treat it like a shiny sticker collection we show off to strangers. Degrees, job titles, certifications, promotions—our society slaps a gold star on those and calls it growth. Meanwhile, the real growth? The messy, awkward, painful kind where you fail, screw up, cry, rage, and then stumble forward? That's quietly shoved into a corner because it doesn't look good on LinkedIn.

But let's tell the truth. Growth looks a lot less like a polished TED Talk and a lot more like a role-playing game where half the quests end in disaster. Every level you gain comes from failing, retrying, and occasionally getting your butt kicked by enemies you didn't even see coming. That heartbreak you barely crawled out of? XP. That time you bombed a job interview so badly you considered faking your own death? XP. That season of life where everything fell apart and you thought you were finished? Surprise—XP.

Life is an RPG with no cheat codes. No infinite lives. No respawn button. You don't get to skip the side quests, either. Every awkward conversation, every mistake, every late-night panic spiral is part of the leveling-up process. The discomfort you're trying to avoid? That's where growth hides.

Here's the kicker: if growth were meant to be easy, puberty wouldn't exist. Growth has always been uncomfortable. The difference is that when you're younger, at least everyone around you knows you're supposed to be awkward. As an adult, you're expected to fake competence while secretly still fumbling in the dark. But don't let the illusion fool you. Nobody levels up gracefully. We all stumble, trip, and grind our way forward.

So this chapter is about learning to embrace that grind. Growth isn't a side hustle or a badge of honor. It's the messy, sometimes humiliating, always necessary process of becoming more alive. And once you stop pretending growth has to look pretty, you can actually enjoy the absurdity of the game.

B: Growth for the 12-Year-Old Explorer

At twelve, growth feels like a full-time job you didn't apply for. Your body is stretching in weird directions, your voice is cracking like a broken microphone, and your brain is flipping between "I want to rule the world" and "I want to hide under my blanket forever." Welcome to Level Awkward.

The good news? Growth at this stage isn't about getting it right. It's about trying. You grow by poking at the world, testing boundaries, asking questions that annoy every adult within a five-mile radius, and failing spectacularly without realizing it's supposed to be embarrassing. You're basically a scientist in sneakers, experimenting with life and jotting down results in invisible ink.

The danger here is when adults mistake your curiosity for distraction. They tell you to "focus" when what they really mean is "stop noticing interesting stuff and do your homework." But the truth is, your curiosity is the engine of growth. Every question you ask, every experiment you try—even the ones that flop—adds XP to your character.

And yes, failure is part of it. You'll bomb tests, lose games, miss cues, and maybe even get rejected by your first crush. Each one will feel like the end of the world. Spoiler: it's not. Those moments are just mini-boss battles designed to teach you resilience. They sting now, but later you'll look back and realize they were tutorials in disguise.

The key at twelve is to keep playing. Don't quit the quest just because you're bad at it at first. Growth isn't about being perfect; it's about collecting the lessons along the way. Every awkward stumble is shaping you into someone stronger, smarter, and weirder—in the best possible way.

So if you feel like you're constantly messing up, good. That's how you know you're growing.

C: Growth for the 18–29 Adventurer

Your twenties are marketed as "the best years of your life." Which is hilarious, because for a lot of people, it feels more like stumbling through a boss fight with a wooden sword and no armor. You're told to figure out who you are, build a career, find love, stay healthy, pay rent, save for retirement, and travel the world—all at once—while pretending you're having fun doing it. If that's not pressure, I don't know what is.

Here's the hard truth: growth in this era rarely looks glamorous. It usually looks like screwing up. You bomb a job interview so badly you consider faking your own death and moving to Peru. You date the wrong person (twice). You spend a semester trying to become a minimalist before realizing you genuinely love owning too many coffee mugs. Each misstep feels like proof that you're failing at adulthood. But what's actually happening is growth disguised as chaos. Every rejection, every bad decision, every awkward "what am I doing with my life" night adds XP to your character sheet.

The danger in your twenties is mistaking *achievement* for growth. Landing the big job, posting the perfect vacation photos, hitting those milestones your family brags about at

Thanksgiving—they look like growth, but they're often just external scorecards. Real growth happens when you wrestle with failure, when you learn how to get back up after the knockdowns.

The irony is that your twenties are supposed to be messy. You're not failing the game; you're in the training grounds. Every mistake is a tutorial, every heartbreak is a skill upgrade, every lost job is a new quest marker. The people who look like they've got it all together? Half of them are faking it, and the other half are quietly falling apart. You're not behind— you're playing the right level.

So instead of panicking about whether you're "growing fast enough," ask yourself: what am I learning? Not what did I achieve, not what did I post online, but what did I actually discover about myself, about others, about life? That's the kind of growth that matters—and that's the kind no one can take from you.

D: Growth for the 30–60 Chaos Survivor

By the time you hit your thirties and beyond, you think you've graduated from life's crash courses. You've got the degree, the job, the partner, the mortgage, maybe the kids, maybe the dog that eats your furniture. You figure growth is for the young— or at least for the people who still have free time and energy. Then life kicks in the door and reminds you: surprise, you're still in class.

Growth at this stage doesn't come from electives you choose. It comes from the assignments you didn't sign up for. Careers change under your feet. Relationships stretch, break, or transform. Parents age, kids grow, your body starts filing complaints you don't remember authorizing. You're tested constantly, and the tests aren't open-book.

Here's the irony: you finally have the wisdom to recognize patterns, but you don't always have the bandwidth to act on them. You know balance matters, but your calendar doesn't care. You know your health is important, but stress has you inhaling lunch at your desk again. You know your relationships need tending, but exhaustion whispers, *maybe tomorrow.* Growth here isn't about knowing better—it's about learning to actually do better, one small adjustment at a time.

And yet, this is where growth gets its richest flavor. You're not experimenting wildly anymore; you're refining. You're learning not just new skills, but new depths—patience, resilience, empathy. The younger you grew by trying new things. The older you grows by sticking with hard things. Showing up to the messy middle of parenting, marriage, work, community—that's growth disguised as ordinary life.

The danger here is stagnation. With so many plates spinning, it's easy to go numb, to coast on autopilot, to think you don't have time to learn anything new. But growth doesn't need giant leaps. It lives in micro-adjustments. Reading a book instead of doomscrolling. Taking a walk instead of another meeting. Apologizing instead of staying defensive.

At this stage, growth isn't about climbing ladders— it's about deepening roots. The real question is: are you evolving with the chaos, or letting it fossilize you? Because one way or another, growth is still happening. The choice is whether it shapes you forward—or just wears you down.

E: Growth for the 60–99 Legacy Keeper

By the time you cross into your sixties, seventies, eighties, and beyond, you've survived enough "growth opportunities" to fill a hundred self-help books. You've learned hard lessons from heartbreaks, jobs gained and lost, friendships stretched thin, health scares, and more family drama than Netflix could dream up. It would be easy to think growth is over now—that you've collected your XP, maxed out your stats, and the rest of the game is just coasting to the credits.

But that's not how growth works. Growth doesn't retire. It just changes its form.

At this stage, growth often looks quieter but deeper. It's not about chasing new titles or achievements. It's about refining your spirit, your perspective, your ability to see the bigger picture. You grow by letting go—of grudges, of expectations, of the illusions you clung to when you were younger. You grow by distilling the chaos of your past into wisdom that others can actually use.

And yes, growth can still be uncomfortable here. The body slows down, health falters, friends fade, the horizon feels closer. Each of those realities forces you to learn again—how to adapt, how to accept, how to find meaning in smaller, slower rhythms. That is growth, even if it doesn't look glamorous.

But there's also a sweetness to growth at this stage. You've lived long enough to know that the real value of learning isn't the degrees or the promotions—it's the stories. The lessons you pass on to your children, your grandchildren, your students, your communities. Growth becomes legacy: not just what you learned, but how you translate it for those who come after you.

The younger you grew by adding layers—skills, knowledge, relationships. The elder you grows by stripping things down to their essence. What really matters? What do I want to leave behind? What's worth carrying forward, and what can I finally set down?

If you've made it to ninety and you're still asking questions, still learning, still curious, then congratulations—you've cracked the secret. Growth was never about getting somewhere. It was always about becoming more fully alive, right until the end.

F: Ibrahim Commentary – Growth Isn't Pretty, It's Awkward

If growth was a clean process, IKEA instructions would make sense the first time. Real growth looks less like the finished product in the glossy catalog and more like that pile of leftover screws, splintered particleboard, and quiet rage on your living room floor at midnight. That's the baseline fact we all forget. Growth has always been awkward, messy, uncomfortable, and usually humiliating. The only reason we think otherwise is because social media turned "personal growth" into a marketing campaign with a filter slapped on top.

Here's the lie: growth looks like success. It looks like a polished LinkedIn announcement about your promotion, or a carefully crafted Instagram post about your yoga retreat in Bali. It looks like the person who seems to be "crushing it" while you're over here eating cold leftovers in yesterday's sweatpants. But that's just the highlight reel. The reality behind the reel? Growth usually looks like crying in the shower, bombing at something new, or failing so hard you consider moving to another country under a fake name.

Every stage of life proves this in its own way. At twelve, growth is pure awkwardness—braces, squeaky voices, tripping over your own feet—and somehow surviving it. At twenty-five, growth is the chaos of bad jobs, bad dates, and bad apartments. At forty-five, it's realizing you can't coast, so you have to keep learning even when you're too tired to care. At ninety-five, it's letting go of the crap you should have dropped decades ago and finally admitting what actually mattered.

And yet we keep treating growth like it's optional. Like it's something you schedule into your Google calendar under "self-improvement," right after spin class. No. Growth is not elective. Growth is mandatory. The only question is whether you're paying attention to it or just pretending you're "fine" while life drags you through the tutorial.

The real secret? Growth is what makes life worth living. Not the polished end result, not the diploma or the job title or the plaque on the wall. The grind itself. The leveling up. The fumbling through quests you don't understand and getting just a little better each time.

You don't need to look graceful while you do it. You don't need to impress anyone. You just need to keep playing. Growth isn't about looking good—it's about becoming more real.

G: Actions – Practicing Growth & Learning

For the 12-Year-Old Explorer
This week, try something new you've never done before. Draw a picture, bake a cake, play a sport, write a story. You don't need to be good at it—in fact, being bad is part of the fun. Growth starts with trying, not perfecting.

For the 18–29 Adventurer
Think of one failure that still stings—a breakup, a rejection, a flop. Write down three things you learned from it. Don't sugarcoat it. Don't turn it into a motivational poster. Just list the raw lessons. Then look at the list and realize: that's XP you earned. That's growth.

For the 30–60 Chaos Survivor
Pick one area of life where you've been stuck. Health, relationships, work, hobbies—whatever's been sitting in limbo. Take one tiny step forward this week. Sign up for a class, take a walk, have the hard conversation, read the first chapter of that book.

Growth isn't about massive leaps. It's about consistent nudges.

For the 60–99 Legacy Keeper

Teach someone a craft you mastered over the years—baking, gardening, woodworking, knitting, fixing a leaky faucet. Your legacy lives in the competence you build in others.

That closes **Chapter 4: Growth & Learning – Leveling Up IRL.**

Chapter 5: Purpose & Contribution – Why Do You Matter?

A: Opening Scene – The Myth of the One True Purpose™

When you're a kid, adults always ask the same question: *"What do you want to be when you grow up?"* It sounds innocent, but baked into it is the assumption that you have one destiny waiting for you, like a Pokémon evolution that unlocks at age twenty-one. Teacher? Doctor? Astronaut? Influencer? Pick carefully, because this is your One True Purpose™.

What nobody bothers to ask is the real question: *"Why do you matter?"*

That's the kicker. From the time you can hold a crayon, you're conditioned to think purpose is about what you *do* for a living. But a job title isn't a purpose. It's just a costume. You can swap it, upgrade it, burn it, or lose it. What sticks—the thing that gives your life weight—isn't the costume. It's what you contribute while you're wearing it.

The modern world makes this even messier. On one hand, we're told to "find ourselves," as if identity and purpose are hiding under a rock somewhere waiting to be discovered. On the other hand, hustle culture screams that if you're not monetizing your hobbies, building a brand, and posting inspirational grindset quotes at 5 a.m., you're wasting your life. God forbid you just enjoy knitting a sweater without trying to turn it into an Etsy empire. No wonder half of us are stressed out of our minds about whether we're "living with purpose."

Here's the reality check: purpose isn't found. It's built. It's not a soulmate you stumble into on a Tuesday; it's a decision you make, over and over again. You take your energy, your quirks, your skills, your love, and you aim them outward. That aiming—that contribution—is what creates purpose.

And contribution doesn't have to be grand. Not everyone is here to cure cancer or build the next billion-dollar app. Sometimes purpose looks like raising kids who aren't assholes. Sometimes it's making your friends laugh until their ribs hurt. Sometimes it's fixing cars so people can get to work, or cooking food that makes a crappy day better, or being the one person who always remembers birthdays. Contribution can be small, quiet, ordinary—and still monumental.

This chapter isn't about convincing you that you've missed your one big calling. It's about showing you that purpose is fluid. It shifts as you grow. What mattered at twelve won't be the same at twenty-five, or forty-five, or ninety-five. But the through-line is always the same: meaning comes from what you give, not what you hoard.

So forget the One True Purpose™. That's a fairy tale. The real story is simpler, messier, and far more satisfying: you matter because you contribute, and those contributions—big or small—are what turn your existence into a life worth remembering.

B: Purpose for the 12-Year-Old Explorer

At twelve, the word "purpose" sounds like something adults argue about in long boring books. You're not trying to solve the meaning of life, you're trying to beat the next video game level, figure out why gym class is torture, and maybe survive middle school without becoming meme material.

And yet, purpose is already shaping you. At this stage, purpose is less about grand destiny and more about *little sparks of mattering.* It's when you tell a joke that makes your friends laugh so hard they can't breathe. It's when you help your parents without being asked, and you see their shoulders drop in relief. It's when you practice drawing, coding, basketball—and realize you're a little better than you were last week. That's purpose-in-training.

The problem is that the world starts telling you your purpose is about achievement. Get good grades. Win the game. Be the best. And while there's nothing wrong with trophies, they're not the whole story. Your real purpose at twelve is curiosity and contribution: discovering what excites you and noticing how you can make life better for the people around you.

That might mean helping a classmate with homework. It might mean standing up when someone gets picked on. It might mean teaching your grandma how to use the TV remote for the hundredth time. These things may not feel epic, but they're the seeds of meaning. You're learning that what you do—even at twelve—ripples outward.

Purpose at this stage is practice. You don't need to know what you want to "be" yet. In fact, you're not supposed to. Your job is to experiment, to play, to try. Collect clues about what lights you up and what helps others. That's how you start building the muscles of contribution.

So don't panic about "finding your purpose." You're twelve. Your purpose is to explore, to learn, and to make small ripples in the lives around you. Those ripples add up.

C: Purpose for the 18–29 Adventurer

Your twenties are the era of the Great Purpose Panic. Everyone—from parents to professors to strangers on LinkedIn—wants to know, *"So what are you doing with your life?"* As if you're supposed to have a PowerPoint presentation ready at all times with a ten-year plan and a mission statement. Spoiler: you're not. And if you do, life will probably laugh in your face and throw you off course anyway.

Here's the trap: you're told that purpose is something you "find." Like it's a treasure chest hidden somewhere, and the only way to unlock it is through hard work, networking, and maybe a semester abroad. So you stress. You compare yourself to people who look like they've figured it all out. You wonder if you're failing because you don't feel a burning passion for your job, or your degree, or whatever random internship you landed.

But purpose at this stage isn't about nailing your forever answer. It's about testing. It's about trying different things, screwing some of them up, and noticing which ones make you feel more alive. Contribution isn't about saving the world in one grand gesture—it's about adding something, anything, that leaves a dent, however small.

Maybe you're building an app nobody downloads. Maybe you're working night shifts just to pay rent. Maybe you're writing songs that only your three friends ever hear. Those things matter, not because they're flashy, but because they're practice. Every failed project teaches you more about what excites you, what drains you, what you can't stop doing even when it's hard.

And yes, relationships are part of this too. You'll give parts of yourself to people who don't keep them. You'll break hearts and have yours broken. And every one of those experiences is a contribution, because they shape you and the people you touch. Messy, painful, real —that's part of your purpose too.

The trick in your twenties is not to confuse "not knowing" with "not growing." Your purpose is evolving while you are. And it doesn't need to look like anyone else's. Forget the treasure chest. Purpose isn't something you find—it's something you build, brick by brick, mistake by mistake, laugh by laugh.

So if you don't have it all figured out yet, good. You're right on schedule.

D: Purpose for the 30–60 Chaos Survivor

By the time you're in your thirties, forties, or fifties, purpose stops feeling like an abstract question and starts feeling like a daily grind. You've got bills to pay, mouths to feed, deadlines to hit, and people counting on you. Congratulations, you are now the infrastructure. And whether you like it or not, your contribution isn't optional—whole systems depend on you to keep moving.

At this stage, purpose often shows up disguised as responsibility. Raising kids, paying the mortgage, showing up to work, caring for aging parents, it's not glamorous, but it's heavy with meaning. Your purpose is baked into the fact that without you, a lot of lives and routines would collapse. But here's the catch: responsibility and purpose aren't the same thing. One can keep you alive, but the other actually makes you feel alive. And if you're not careful, the weight of responsibility can smother any sense of deeper contribution.

This is where the famous "midlife crisis" comes in. You wake up one day and wonder: is this it? Is my purpose just being the human equivalent of duct tape, holding everything together? That itch for something more—whether it's a new hobby, a career change, or, yes, buying a sports car—isn't about immaturity. It's about purpose knocking on the door, reminding you that you're allowed to grow beyond your obligations.

Contribution at this stage doesn't have to be world changing. It can be raising decent kids. It can be mentoring younger colleagues. It can be creating something—writing, painting, fixing, gardening—that outlives the chaos of your to-do list. The point isn't scale, it's intention. Purpose grows when you stop asking "What do I have to do?" and start asking "What do I want my life to add up to?"

So yes, these years are heavy. They're chaotic, exhausting, and sometimes brutally unfair. But they're also rich with opportunities to define your contribution. You don't have to abandon your responsibilities to live with purpose. You just have to weave purpose into them—by noticing the ways your actions ripple outward, by choosing which obligations actually align with your deeper values, and by daring, even in the chaos, to claim something for yourself.

Because if you wait until retirement to live with purpose, you've missed decades of chances to matter.

E: Purpose for the 60–99 Legacy Keeper

By the time you reach your sixties and beyond, the word "purpose" shifts again. It's no longer about climbing ladders or checking boxes. It's about looking back at the mountain you've already climbed and asking: *What did it all mean? What do I leave behind?*

At this stage, purpose often feels less urgent but more profound. You've carried families, careers, friendships, responsibilities—and now you get to sift through it all to see what really mattered. Spoiler:

67

it's usually not the titles, trophies, or paychecks. Those gather dust. The purpose that lingers is the love you gave, the people you raised, the moments you showed up when it counted.

Contribution here often takes the form of storytelling. Passing on wisdom, sharing lessons, keeping traditions alive. A grandparent telling a grandchild about the time they marched, or built, or failed, or loved badly and then learned better—that's contribution. That's continuity. You may not feel like you're "building" anymore, but you're still shaping the future through the stories and love you leave behind.

Of course, these years can also bring doubt. Did I do enough? Did I matter? That's the haunting side of reflection. But here's the truth: if you've touched even a handful of lives, if you've made people laugh, if you've taught something worth remembering, if you've loved in a way that left a mark—then yes, you mattered. And that contribution ripples forward long after you're gone.

Purpose at this stage becomes less about doing and more about being. Being present. Being honest. Being generous with your stories, your time, your patience. And sometimes, being at peace with the fact that you won't tie up every loose end. That's okay. Nobody does.

So if you're in your seventies, eighties, nineties, still asking "Why do I matter?"—remember this: you matter because you existed, and because your existence touched others. And that's contribution enough to echo into the future.

F: Ken Commentary – Purpose Isn't Found, It's Built

If purpose were hiding somewhere, it would be in an IKEA warehouse: confusing instructions, missing screws, and somehow you always end up with a piece left over. That's how most people treat it—like there's a One True Purpose™ out there, and if they don't "find" it by 25, they're doomed to a meaningless existence. Spoiler: that's garbage.

Purpose isn't a soulmate. It's not a treasure chest. It doesn't come with a certificate or a drumroll. Purpose is built, day by day, out of whatever scraps of energy, love, and skill you can throw at the world. Contribution is how you turn that pile of scraps into something that matters.

But we live in a culture obsessed with grandiosity. You don't just need a purpose—you need a TED Talk about it. A side hustle. A social media brand where your "authenticity" is curated down to the latte art. Hustle culture has turned purpose into a competition, and it's exhausting. Meanwhile, the truth is sitting in plain sight: you matter because of what you give, not how shiny it looks on Instagram.

Every stage of life proves this in its own ridiculous way. At twelve, your purpose is to explore and start helping in small ways. At twenty-five, it's to experiment and screw up until you figure out what feels real. At forty-five, it's to balance responsibility with intentional contribution, instead of letting obligation eat your soul. And at ninety, it's to pass on stories and wisdom that outlive you. None of

69

those require viral fame, six figures, or a bestselling memoir. They just require showing up.

The kicker? Purpose isn't static. It mutates. It grows with you. If you're waiting for the lightning bolt moment where your "real" purpose reveals itself, you'll be waiting forever. The only way to have a purpose is to *choose one, live it, and adjust as you go.*

So here's the truth bomb: you already matter. You matter because you're here. You matter because you've touched lives in ways you probably don't even realize. And your purpose isn't out there waiting— it's already in motion every time you give something to someone else, every time you contribute even the smallest act of care, humor, or effort.

Forget finding. Start building.

G: Actions – Practicing Purpose & Contribution

For the 12-Year-Old Explorer
Do one small helpful thing this week without being asked. Help a parent, a friend, a teacher—even something tiny. Notice how it feels to make life easier for someone else. That's contribution in its purest form.

For the 18–29 Adventurer
Grab a notebook or your phone. Write down three things that energize you and three things that drain you. Circle one energizing thing and do more of it this week. Purpose isn't revealed in a vision quest— it grows from noticing what lights you up and acting on it.

For the 30–60 Chaos Survivor

Pick one responsibility you already do—parenting, mentoring, your work—and ask yourself, *how is this contributing?* Write down your answer. Then double down on that one meaningful angle instead of trying to be everything to everyone. Purpose gets sharper when you stop scattering yourself.

For the 60–99 Legacy Keeper

Write down the three most important life lessons you've learned—not as long stories, but as simple, powerful sentences. This is your "legacy manifesto." Share it with your family or a mentee.

And with that, **Chapter 5: Purpose & Contribution – Why Do You Matter?** is complete.

Chapter 6: Joy & Experience

The Art of Actually Enjoying the Ride

A: Opening Scene – Joy Isn't Dessert, It's the Meal

Somewhere along the way, humans decided joy was optional. Like dessert. You only get to taste it after you've eaten your vegetables, done your homework, filed your taxes, and proven you're a responsible adult. Then, *maybe*, if there's time, you can have fun. Joy becomes the bonus round. The reward for suffering through "real life."

Which is insane. Joy isn't dessert. Joy is the meal. It's the thing that makes all the other chewing, grinding, and slogging worth it. Without joy, survival is just existing. Without joy, growth is just pain. Without joy, purpose feels like a chore. Strip away laughter, awe, and delight, and life is basically one long spreadsheet of obligations.

The tragedy is, our culture has managed to make joy feel guilty. If you're not productive every second, you're wasting time. Taking a walk? Lazy. Playing a video game? Childish. Laughing too much at a meme? Irresponsible. Even vacations have been rebranded as "networking opportunities" or "content creation trips." Apparently, even joy needs a business plan now.

And then there's consumer culture, which hijacks joy completely. Ads scream: "Buy this, and you'll be happy!" Spoiler: you won't. That gadget, that car, that subscription service—they give you a dopamine blip, not joy. Real joy doesn't come from swiping a credit card. It comes from moments that are usually free: a ridiculous belly laugh, a sunset that makes you shut up for once, music that hits so hard you feel like your bones are vibrating.

The point is this: joy isn't extra. It's essential. It's not something you "earn" after enough suffering. It's the fuel that makes the suffering survivable, the chaos bearable, the purpose meaningful. Nobody looks back at their life and says, "You know what I wish I did more of? Worked late." They say, "I wish I laughed more, traveled more, danced more, loved more."

So this chapter is about reclaiming joy—not as a luxury, but as a birthright. And it's about reminding you that experiences are the actual currency of meaning. The ride *is* the point. So buckle up, because we're about to talk about how joy saves your life in ways no productivity hack ever will.

B: Joy for the 12-Year-Old Explorer

At twelve, joy is supposed to be your job description. Play, laugh, get curious, repeat. The world is still wide open, every day is an experiment, and joy doesn't need an excuse. You can spend hours building a Lego city, laughing at the dumbest joke with your best friend, or running around outside until you collapse in a sweaty heap. That's joy—and it's not a waste of time. It's the work of being alive.

Here's the catch: adults start training you out of joy early. "Stop goofing off." "Focus." "Be serious." Suddenly, joy becomes something you sneak in between assignments, like contraband. You're told that grades and responsibilities are what matter most, and play is just a reward for finishing "real work." Which is ridiculous, because at twelve, joy is where most of your real learning happens.

Think about it: the times you laugh hardest with friends, the moments you lose yourself in a hobby, the pure silliness of inventing a game nobody else understands—that's where you discover creativity, connection, and resilience. You're learning how to interact, how to solve problems, how to stay curious. Joy is a classroom disguised as fun.

The danger is that if you start believing joy doesn't matter, you'll carry that lie into adulthood. You'll grow up thinking fun is frivolous, and by the time you're thirty, you'll feel guilty for doing anything that isn't "productive." Which is how you end up with miserable grown-ups who work themselves into the ground and wonder why life feels empty.

So at twelve, your mission isn't to "find" joy—it's to protect it. Play with no agenda. Laugh loudly. Notice the weirdness of the world. Ask ridiculous questions. And don't let anyone convince you that joy is a waste of time. It's not. It's fuel.

Because the truth is, if you can hold onto the art of play now, you'll carry it with you forever. And that's one of the greatest gifts you can give your future self.

C: Joy for the 18–29 Adventurer

In your twenties, joy feels like it should be everywhere. Late-night road trips, concerts where you scream the lyrics until your throat gives out, friendships so intense they feel like family, first loves, first heartbreaks, the thrill of being free to make your own choices. If childhood joy is about play, young adult joy is about *exploration.* Every experience feels like it might matter forever.

And sometimes it does. You'll remember those 2 a.m. diner runs for the rest of your life. You'll remember the song that became the soundtrack of a whole season. You'll remember the laugh that made you fall in love. These are the bright threads that stitch your twenties together.

But here's the danger: joy at this stage can get hijacked. You're broke, you're stressed, you're comparing your messy reality to everyone else's highlight reel, and joy starts to feel like something other people have. So you numb out. Binge-watch, scroll endlessly, drink too much, hook up with people you don't care about—chasing quick hits of dopamine instead of real joy. It's not that those things are evil, but they're not the same as experiences that actually feed you.

Joy in your twenties requires discernment. It's about asking: *Does this make me feel more alive, or emptier afterward?* Joy that drains you isn't joy—it's distraction. Joy that fills you is the kind that lingers, the kind you can recall years later with a smile.

And here's the secret: you don't have to wait until you're "successful" to deserve joy. You don't need six figures in the bank or a verified checkmark to take a trip, dance all night, or sit in the park laughing with friends. Joy is available in the middle of the mess. In fact, the mess is where it matters most.

So yes, explore. Try things. Say yes to experiences. Screw up, laugh about it, and keep going. But pay attention to which kinds of joy leave you richer, not poorer. Because in your twenties, joy isn't just about having fun—it's about learning what truly lights you up so you don't spend your thirties mistaking noise for meaning.

D: Joy for the 30–60 Chaos Survivor

By the time you hit your thirties, forties, and fifties, joy is no longer waiting around every corner. It doesn't knock on your door like it did in your twenties. You've got jobs, bills, kids, aging parents, aging knees, and a calendar that looks like a sadistic puzzle designed to keep you too tired to rebel. Somewhere along the line, joy got demoted from "daily necessity" to "maybe, if I get around to it after laundry."

And yet, this is the stage where joy matters most— because without it, the chaos eats you alive. Without joy, your life becomes nothing but obligations, deadlines, and grocery lists. Without joy, you start to believe your only role is worker, parent, provider, caretaker—human infrastructure with a pulse. That's not living. That's maintenance.

The danger here is that you start thinking joy has to be big to count. Exotic vacations, expensive hobbies, bucket-list achievements. Those are nice, sure, but they're not the essence of joy. Real joy at this stage often hides in the small stuff: your kid saying something hilarious, your partner making coffee just the way you like it, singing badly in the car with the windows down, laughing with a friend over how ridiculous adulthood actually is.

Joy is the rebellion against burnout. It's the crack in the chaos where you remember, *Oh right, I'm alive.* And it doesn't take hours you don't have. It takes moments you choose to notice. A deep breath on the porch before you walk back inside. A joke told in the middle of a stressful meeting. Five minutes playing your guitar, even if it gathers dust the rest of the week.

Here's the truth: if you wait for the chaos to die down before you allow yourself joy, you'll be waiting forever. Joy isn't what comes after you handle life. Joy is what keeps you from drowning in it.

So schedule it. Protect it. Treat it like oxygen, not dessert. Because in these years, joy isn't optional—it's survival with flavor.

E: Joy for the 60–99 Legacy Keeper

By the time you reach your sixties and beyond, joy stops being about chasing and starts being about savoring. You don't need the all-nighters, the epic trips, or the Instagram-worthy adventures to feel alive anymore. Joy now lives in the small, familiar, ordinary moments that reveal themselves as extraordinary when you slow down enough to notice.

Joy is your grandchild's laugh as they discover something for the first time. It's coffee shared on a quiet morning with someone you love. It's music from your youth that still makes you hum along. It's telling a story from decades ago and watching the younger generation lean in like it's brand-new.

At this stage, joy and gratitude often blend into one. You start realizing that joy isn't about how much you do—it's about how deeply you appreciate what's in front of you. A good meal, a warm blanket, the sound of rain—all of these can glow with meaning if you're awake enough to let them.

But here's the other side: joy can get complicated when loss starts stacking up. Friends pass. Health wavers. The world speeds on without you. It's easy to feel like joy belongs to the younger. That's the lie. Joy isn't youth's property—it's humanity's. And in these years, joy takes on its sharpest edge because you know how precious each moment is.

Contribution ties in here too. Sharing joy becomes a gift you hand down. Your stories, your laughter, your wisdom—they become torches lighting the path for others. The joy you savor becomes the joy you multiply.

So if you're in your later decades, your mission isn't to chase joy like you're twenty again. It's to savor it, amplify it, and pass it on. Because at this stage, joy isn't just fuel for you—it's a legacy for everyone who comes after.

F: Ibrahim Commentary – Stop Treating Joy Like It's Extra Credit

Here's the cultural scam: we treat joy like it's our leftover vacation days, a scarce resource you're almost afraid to use, something you have to hoard for a 'special occasion' that never seems to arrive. We act as if the universe is an HR department that will only approve your fun after you've filed the proper paperwork of suffering. Joy becomes the reward for being a good little worker bee. Which is ridiculous, because without joy, all the other stuff is pointless. Who cares if you built the perfect resume if you never laughed so hard your stomach hurt?

The truth is, joy is not extra credit. Joy is the syllabus. It's the part of the human operating system that keeps us from turning into hollow-eyed productivity machines. And yet, our culture guilt-trips us out of it. If you take a break, you're lazy. If you play, you're childish. If you laugh too much, you're not "serious" enough. Meanwhile, half the serious people are quietly miserable, and the other half are medicating their misery by buying stuff they don't need.

Every stage of life knows this, in its own language. At twelve, joy is pure play—silly, messy, and essential. At twenty-five, joy is exploration, the late-night chaos you'll remember forever. At forty-five, joy is survival fuel, stolen in moments before the grind eats you whole. And at ninety, joy is savoring—the

79

slow, rich glow of noticing what's left. Different flavors, same truth: joy is the proof that life was worth the trouble.

Here's the kicker: joy isn't always convenient. It doesn't schedule itself neatly between your meetings. You have to choose it. Protect it. Fight for it. And sometimes, create it in the middle of mess. Joy isn't what happens after you finish living. Joy is the living.

So let's stop pretending joy is frivolous. It's not. It's medicine. It's rebellion. It's oxygen. And the only people who will ever try to convince you otherwise are the ones who already forgot how to feel it themselves.

G: Actions – Practicing Joy & Experience

For the 12-Year-Old Explorer
Set aside one hour this week for pure play. No homework, no goals, no grades. Build, draw, play tag, make noise, invent something silly. Pay attention to how alive you feel when you're not worried about "doing it right."

For the 18–29 Adventurer
Plan one experience that excites you—something that's just for you, not for Instagram. A concert, a hike, a road trip, a night with friends. Put it on the calendar and protect it like it's a final exam. Because joy doesn't happen by accident when you're this busy—it happens when you claim it.

For the 30–60 Chaos Survivor
Choose one joy ritual and lock it in this week. A

family dinner, a weekly hobby, a silly game with your kids, even a solo coffee at your favorite café. Treat it like an unbreakable meeting with your soul. Small, repeatable joys are the antidote to chaos.

For the 60–99 Legacy Keeper
Create a photo album, a scrapbook, or a digital folder titled "The Good Stuff." Fill it with pictures and mementos of joy from your life and share the stories behind the images. This makes legacy a tangible artifact of happiness.

That completes **Chapter 6: Joy & Experience – The Art of Actually Enjoying the Ride.**

Chapter 7: Suffering & Transcendence – The Pain That Shapes Us

A: Opening Scene – Congratulations, You Suffer

Congratulations: you suffer. Welcome to the species. You might have thought you were signing up for the deluxe package—sunsets, laughter, Netflix binges—but buried in the fine print of being alive is the unavoidable truth: you're going to hurt. Physically, emotionally, spiritually—pick your poison. Nobody escapes.

And yet, if you scroll through Instagram or flip on a commercial, you'd think suffering is optional. Everyone else looks like they're living their best lives, smiling through perfect vacations and artisanal coffee foam. Spoiler: they're not. Behind the filters, everyone's carrying something—loss, loneliness, anxiety, grief, disappointment. They're just better at hiding it, or distracting themselves until it leaks out sideways.

Buddha said, "Life is suffering," and he didn't mean it in a bummer, emo-teen kind of way. He meant that suffering is baked into existence. Things break. People die. Bodies fail. Relationships shatter. Dreams collapse. Even if you win the lottery, you'll still age, ache, and eventually leave it all behind. Rich or poor, young or old, the pain eventually finds you.

Our modern world hates that truth. We're obsessed with comfort. We numb ourselves with screens, shopping carts, substances, noise—anything to avoid sitting in pain. And sure, distraction works for a while. But suffering is like a debt collector: you can dodge the calls, but it'll find you eventually, and the interest just keeps piling up.

Here's the twist: suffering isn't just inevitable. It's useful. It's the great equalizer, the thing that cracks us open, humbles us, teaches us empathy, forces us to grow. Nobody likes pain, but most of the deepest lessons we carry—the ones that actually shape us—come from the times we didn't get what we wanted.

So this chapter is about leaning into that uncomfortable truth. Suffering isn't the enemy. It's the forge. The heat that reshapes you. The mud you crawl through that makes the sunrise mean something. You don't transcend pain by avoiding it; you transcend it by facing it, enduring it, and somehow making something out of it.

Welcome to the part of life nobody asked for, but everybody needs.

B: Suffering for the 12-Year-Old Explorer

At twelve, suffering feels enormous. Your best friend stops talking to you. You get picked last for the team. Someone makes fun of your clothes, your braces, your voice cracking at the worst possible moment. You fail a test you studied for. You get grounded. To an adult, these things might look

83

small. But to you, they're everything. At twelve, pain isn't practice—it's the whole game.

And here's the thing: it *is* real. Don't let anyone tell you, "You'll get over it" as if it doesn't matter. Of course you'll get over it eventually, but right now, it hurts. Your brain and body react to rejection, embarrassment, and loss the same way they react to bigger traumas later in life. Your heart races, your stomach knots, your face burns. It's not fake. It's biology.

But here's the secret adults wish they'd understood when they were your age: every one of these hurts is a training session. Every time you recover from a fight with a friend, a bad grade, or the sting of being left out, you're building muscles you'll use for the rest of your life. Muscles of resilience. Muscles of empathy. Muscles that teach you: *I can survive this.*

Think of it like video games. Early levels throw smaller enemies at you, not because they don't matter, but because you need practice before the bigger bosses show up. Getting laughed at in gym class? That's a mini-boss. Failing math? Another mini-boss. Learning to recover now means when the harder battles show up later—loss, heartbreak, real grief—you've got some XP already banked.

It doesn't make the pain less real. But it means the pain has purpose. At twelve, your suffering teaches you that feelings pass, wounds heal, and life keeps moving. It's the first lesson in the truth you'll keep relearning: pain may knock you down, but it doesn't get to keep you there.

So when something hurts at twelve, don't dismiss it. Feel it. Talk about it. Write it down. Let yourself learn from it. These are your first scars, and they're not signs of weakness. They're your training badges.

C: Suffering for the 18–29 Adventurer

Your twenties are marketed as freedom, fun, and self-discovery. What they don't tell you is that "self-discovery" often feels like getting punched in the gut by reality over and over again. You suffer through rejections—jobs, relationships, friendships that don't last. You suffer through money stress, wondering how rent costs half your paycheck. You suffer through figuring out who you are while everyone else looks like they've already nailed it. Spoiler: they haven't.

The suffering here is real and sharp. First big heartbreaks. First dreams collapsing. First time you realize "finding yourself" isn't a vacation in Bali—it's crying on the bathroom floor at 2 a.m., wondering if you're screwing up your one shot at life. It feels personal, like you're failing while everyone else is thriving. But here's the truth: you're not broken. You're just in the forge.

Suffering in your twenties is the fire that burns away illusions. The illusion that life is fair. The illusion that love always lasts. The illusion that hard work guarantees success. Each time something shatters, you grieve. But in that grief, something else is born—resilience, clarity, depth.

The danger is numbing out. Distracting yourself with endless scrolling, hookups you don't care about, drinking until you forget. And sure, distraction feels good for a night. But suffering you don't face just waits for you in the morning. Pain is patient. It'll sit there, sipping coffee, until you're ready to deal with it.

The transcendence comes when you stop treating suffering as proof you're failing, and start treating it as evidence you're alive and learning. That rejection? It taught you what you don't want. That breakup? It showed you what love should really feel like. That dead-end job? It made you hungry for something better.

The truth is, nobody gets through their twenties without scars. But scars aren't shame—they're proof you showed up. And every scar carries wisdom you'll use for the rest of your life.

So if you're in your twenties, suffering doesn't mean you're off track. It means you're in the thick of the training ground. And while it hurts now, you're collecting the resilience and empathy that will shape who you become.

D: Suffering for the 30–60 Chaos Survivor

By the time your back goes out more than you do, suffering isn't just a surprise guest—it's a roommate. It doesn't just show up once in a while; it lingers. These are the years when the big stuff hits: losing parents, struggling through divorce, raising kids while trying not to lose your sanity, watching careers stall, facing illnesses you thought only "older people" got. The smaller pains of youth feel like practice rounds compared to the heaviness of real adult suffering.

This is where pain feels relentless. You're carrying more than you thought possible—deadlines, bills, caretaking, the ache of grief, the weight of being the one everyone else relies on. Sometimes suffering doesn't feel like a dramatic event; it feels like exhaustion that never lifts. It's burnout, loneliness in a crowded house, waking up with a knot in your chest and pretending you're fine because people are counting on you.

And here's the truth you don't want but need to hear: this is also where meaning deepens. These are the years when suffering forces you to grow in directions you never asked for—patience, endurance, compassion. You discover strength you didn't know you had, not because you wanted to, but because you had no choice. That doesn't make the suffering noble—it still hurts like hell—but it does mean it isn't wasted.

The danger here is collapse into numbness. You get so used to carrying the weight that you stop noticing how heavy it is. You power through, you perform, you endure—and somewhere along the line, you forget you're human. You forget that pain doesn't have to be carried alone. And that forgetting is what breaks people.

Transcendence here isn't about "rising above" the pain like some spiritual superhero. It's about transforming it. Letting grief teach you empathy.

Letting failure strip away pride and leave you humble. Letting burnout remind you that joy matters, not just duty. The cracks suffering creates can also let the light in—if you're willing to stop pretending you're unbreakable.

At this stage, suffering is no longer a side quest. It's part of the main storyline. And while you don't get to choose when or how it arrives, you do get to choose whether it hardens you into stone or softens you into someone who sees more, feels more, and gives more.

E: Suffering for the 60–99 Legacy Keeper

By the time you reach your sixties, seventies, eighties, and beyond, suffering changes its shape again. It's not just the setbacks of youth or the chaos of midlife—it's the long, slow process of letting go. You suffer as your body slows down, as aches become companions, as independence begins to slip away. You suffer losses more often now: friends passing, loved ones gone, whole chapters of your life closing. Grief isn't an occasional storm; it's a recurring season.

And yet, in these years, something else begins to shine through suffering: transcendence. You've lived long enough to see that pain isn't the end of the story. It bends you, yes, but it also shapes you. Loss sharpens love. Fragility makes every moment glow brighter. Knowing time is short gives life an intensity you didn't notice when you thought you had forever.

The temptation here is despair—believing suffering has the final word. But many in this stage discover something deeper: acceptance. Not passive resignation, but an active choosing to savor what remains. A sunrise. A child's laughter. A memory that still brings tears and joy in equal measure. These small things become enormous, because you understand how precious they are.

This is also the stage where your suffering becomes someone else's compass. When you share the story of how you survived loss, endured illness, or kept going when you thought you couldn't—you offer hope. You prove to the generations after you that pain is survivable. That meaning can be made out of it. That scars aren't shame—they're maps.

And when death draws closer, suffering brings its final lesson: everything ends. But that doesn't erase the meaning of what came before. In fact, it makes every act of love, every laugh, every contribution more sacred. Transcendence here isn't about escaping pain—it's about embracing the beauty that exists alongside it, even in the shadow of the inevitable.

At this stage, suffering doesn't define you. What defines you is the way you've transformed it—into wisdom, into compassion, into stories that will outlast you. That's transcendence: not a life without pain, but a life that alchemizes pain into something worth passing on.

F: Ken Commentary – Pain Isn't a Glitch, It's the Code

Here's the hard truth nobody wants to print on a Hallmark card: suffering isn't a glitch in life's programming—it's the code itself. You don't get to opt out. Congratulations, you're human: you will hurt. But instead of facing that reality, we've built an entire industry trying to duct-tape a smile over it.

You know what I'm talking about—those "Good vibes only!" posters, the influencers chirping about gratitude journaling while hiding their panic attacks, and that one aunt who tells you to 'just choose happiness' when your life is on fire, as if you hadn't thought of that, the corporate wellness emails telling you to "breathe through the stress" while dumping another twelve projects on your desk. That's not transcendence. That's denial with a ring light.

The truth is that suffering is the most democratic experience in existence. Doesn't matter if you're rich or broke, twelve or ninety, single or married, saint or jerk—pain is coming for you. The flavors vary (heartbreak, burnout, grief, illness, loneliness), but the menu is the same for everyone. That's the hidden connection: we're all bleeding under our armor, even if we pretend otherwise.

Every stage of life has its brand of suffering. At twelve, the pain feels world-ending even if it's a bad grade or losing a friend. At twenty-five, it's the gut-punch of rejection, failure, and identity crises. At forty-five, it's the grind of endless responsibility and grief stacked like unpaid bills. And at ninety, it's the ache of loss, the weight of decline, and the sharp knowledge that endings are near. Different costumes, same play.

But here's the secret sauce: suffering isn't just pain—it's transformation. It's the forge that burns away illusions and leaves you with something raw, real, and often uncomfortably honest. Pain teaches empathy. Failure breeds humility. Loss makes love sharper. Even grief, as cruel as it feels, reminds you that you cared deeply enough to hurt.

Transcendence doesn't mean floating above the pain like some serene monk. It means walking through the fire and dragging meaning out of the ashes. It means saying, "Yes, this broke me—but it also remade me." That doesn't erase the hurt, but it does redeem it.

So next time someone hands you a "just stay positive!" platitude, feel free to laugh. Suffering isn't something you bypass with a motivational quote. It's something you endure, wrestle with, and eventually transform into a story worth telling. That's transcendence—not denial, not avoidance, but alchemy.

Pain isn't proof you're failing. Pain is the proof you're alive.

G: Actions – Practicing Transcendence Through Suffering

For the 12-Year-Old Explorer

When something hurts—whether it's a fight with a friend, a bad grade, or feeling left out—don't shove it down. Write about it in a notebook, draw it, or talk to someone you trust. Notice how naming the pain makes it shrink. That's your first step in learning that pain doesn't control you.

For the 18–29 Adventurer
Pick one past hurt that still stings—a breakup, rejection, failure. Write down three things it taught you. Maybe it gave you clarity, resilience, or showed you what you don't want. That lesson is your badge of transcendence—proof that suffering wasn't wasted.

For the 30–60 Chaos Survivor
Choose one healthy practice for dealing with suffering instead of numbing it. Therapy, journaling, long walks, prayer, meditation, even a brutally honest talk with a friend. Put it into your week, the way you'd schedule a meeting. Because processing pain is just as important as paying bills, it keeps you alive.

For the 60–99 Legacy Keeper
Offer the legacy of reconciliation. Make one phone call or write one letter to mend a fence or forgive an old grudge. Leaving behind a legacy of peace is one of the most powerful things you can do.

That completes **Chapter 7: Suffering & Transcendence – The Pain That Shapes Us.**

Chapter 8: Ethics & Responsibility – How to Live Without Being a Jerk

A: Opening Scene – Everyone Thinks They're the Good Guy

Here's a universal truth: everyone thinks they're the good guy. Everyone. The corporate executive dumping toxic sludge into a river? He'll tell you it's "job creation." The politician slashing social programs? She'll call it "fiscal responsibility." The neighbor who refuses to pick up their dog's poop? In their mind, it's "fertilizer." The activist who tweets 'BE KIND' in all caps right before screaming at a barista for using oat milk instead of almond? They're just 'passionate.'

Nobody wakes up, twirls a mustache in the mirror, and says, "Time to be the villain today." We all justify our choices, even the crappy ones. Which is why ethics is such a slippery beast. It's not about the story you tell yourself—it's about the impact you actually have on other people.

And that's where responsibility comes in. Responsibility is ethics with boots on. It's the proof that you care enough to back up your values with action. Without responsibility, ethics is just a motivational poster on the wall of a break room everyone ignores.

But here's the kicker: we live in an age of ethical shortcuts. Companies slap "eco-friendly" on a plastic bottle and call it a day. Influencers preach mindfulness while screaming at waiters off-camera. People tweet furious threads about justice while ghosting their own friends. We've mastered the art of performative ethics—looking virtuous without doing the hard, boring work of responsibility.

And yet, meaning doesn't come from looking good. It comes from living good—or at least trying to. Nobody's perfect. We all screw up, cut corners, and tell little lies. The point isn't to be flawless. The point is to catch yourself when you're slipping, own it, and course-correct before you become the villain in someone else's story.

This chapter isn't about wagging fingers or laying down commandments. It's about exploring why ethics and responsibility aren't just rules, they're scaffolding of meaning. They're how you matter not just to yourself, but to others. Without them, your life might be fun, flashy, and full of stuff—but it won't leave much behind except messes other people have to clean up.

So let's talk about how to live without being a jerk. Spoiler: it's harder than you think.

B: Ethics for the 12-Year-Old Explorer

At twelve, ethics usually boils down to one word: *fair.* You don't need a philosophy degree to know when someone cuts in line, cheats at a game, or takes more than their share—it feels wrong. Your whole body reacts. That sense of justice is your first moral compass, and it's sharper than you think.

Responsibility shows up too, usually disguised as chores or schoolwork. Take out the trash. Do your homework. Don't let your little brother set the couch on fire. None of these tasks seem like they have much to do with ethics, but they're actually training you. You're learning that promises matter, that actions have consequences, that other people depend on you to keep things from falling apart.

Of course, this is also the age when bending the truth feels like an Olympic sport. Did you *really* finish your homework? Did you *really* not eat the last cookie? Did the dog *really* eat your project? At twelve, honesty gets tested daily, and every lie you tell is a mini experiment in "Can I get away with this?" The answer is: sometimes. But the bigger answer is: every time you lie, you chip away at trust—and trust is the currency of belonging.

The big lesson here is simple: ethics isn't about following rules because adults said so. It's about noticing how your choices affect people around you. If you share, everyone gets more. If you cheat, everyone gets less. If you keep your word, people start trusting you. If you break it, people stop.

At twelve, responsibility can feel like a drag, and fairness can feel like a battle cry ("That's not fair!" might be your favorite phrase). But underneath the complaints, you're learning the foundation of meaning: life is better when you treat others with respect, and when you can be counted on.

95

Nobody expects you to be perfect at this stage. You're going to mess up. You'll lie, you'll slack off, you'll blame your sibling for something you did. But every mistake is a chance to learn. And the sooner you realize ethics isn't about punishment, it's about connection, the sooner you start building the kind of life people actually want to share with you.

C: Ethics for the 18–29 Adventurer

Your twenties are the first-time ethics stop being a theory and start being a bill that comes due. In school, bad decisions usually meant detention or grounding. Out here? They can cost you jobs, relationships, reputations, money—and sometimes all of the above in one spectacular flameout.

This is the age where you test boundaries. You tell yourself, *I'll cut this corner just once. I'll ghost them instead of having the hard conversation. I'll fudge my résumé a little because everyone else does.* And maybe you get away with it. But here's the trap: every time you dodge responsibility, you're not just risking consequences, you're shaping who you are becoming.

Relationships are ground zero for ethical lessons in your twenties. Do you tell the truth even when it's awkward? Do you own up to mistakes or hide them? Do you treat people like placeholders until something "better" comes along? Responsibility here isn't just about not being a jerk—it's about realizing the kind of partner, friend, and colleague you're building yourself into.

Work life adds another layer. Do you steal credit or share it? Do you speak up when something shady is happening, or do you stay quiet to keep the paycheck? Every job, even the soul-crushing ones, puts your ethics under the microscope. And the choices you make—big or small—start etching a pattern that sticks.

The myth in your twenties is that you're the exception. *Sure, other people have to play by the rules, but I'm smart enough to game the system.* That's the fast lane to becoming the villain in someone else's story. Responsibility at this stage is learning you're not above it. You don't get a free pass just because you're young and figuring things out.

Here's the hopeful part: you're also laying foundations. Every time you own a mistake instead of dodging it, you build trust. Every time you choose integrity over shortcuts, you strengthen your reputation. Every time you show up when you could have flaked, you prove to yourself and others that you can be counted on. And trust us—that pays dividends far bigger than the temporary win of cheating the system.

In your twenties, ethics isn't about being perfect. It's about catching yourself, correcting yourself, and realizing responsibility is the glue that holds real adulthood together.

D: Ethics for the 30–60 Chaos Survivor

Once you've logged enough hours to reach the main campaign of adulthood, ethics isn't a classroom debate or a late-night dorm argument, it's a daily test. And the test has consequences that don't just land on you. Your choices ripple outward into your family, your workplace, your friendships, your community. People are depending on you now. The margin for selfishness shrinks.

This is the stage where responsibility becomes inescapable. Kids need you to show up. Partners need you to keep promises. Employees or coworkers need you to be honest, competent, and fair. Communities need you to contribute instead of hiding behind excuses. You're no longer experimenting with ethics—you're living inside the results of your past choices.

And here's where the tension kicks in: pressure. When the bills pile up, when the job is on the line, when the marriage feels fragile, ethics gets tested. It's easy to cut corners, to justify, to say, "I'll fix it later." It's also easy to slip into hypocrisy—preaching responsibility to your kids while breaking your own rules, telling your team to be honest while covering up your own mistakes. Kids, by the way, have hypocrisy radar sharper than a bloodhound. They'll spot it in a heartbeat.

The real danger here is exhaustion. When you're juggling so many responsibilities, it's tempting to think ethics is optional. You start saying, "I don't have time to deal with this the right way—I'll do it the fast way." And while that shortcut might save a little time today, it costs you trust tomorrow. And trust is a lot harder to rebuild than a bank account.

But here's the hope: ethics at this stage doesn't have to be about perfection—it's about consistency. It's about showing up, owning mistakes, keeping promises, and refusing to let the chaos erode your integrity. The smallest choices—telling the truth when it's hard, apologizing when you're wrong, treating people with respect even when you're tired— are the ones that define you most.

By this point, people around you have seen enough to know who you really are. Ethics isn't your theory anymore, it's your reputation. And responsibility isn't punishment—it's proof you matter to people who are counting on you.

E: Ethics for the 60–99 Legacy Keeper

By the time you reach your sixties and beyond, ethics stops being a set of abstract rules or workplace dilemmas—it becomes a mirror. You look back over decades of choices and ask: *What kind of person was I? What kind of mark did I leave?*

At this stage, responsibility isn't just about paying bills or showing up to work—it's about legacy. Did you live with integrity, or did you leave a trail of broken promises? Did you teach your children and grandchildren honesty, or did they learn hypocrisy from watching you? Did you make amends where you could, or did you let pride harden into silence?

This is also when the gray areas of ethics come back to haunt you—or heal you. The lies you told, the shortcuts you took, the ways you treated people—by now, the results are visible. Some bonds will have survived because you chose honesty and care. Others may be fractured because you didn't. Responsibility in these years often looks like reconciliation: picking up the phone, writing the letter, saying the apology you should've said decades ago.

And here's the gift: it's not too late. Ethics isn't about never making mistakes, it's about facing them, even years later. You may not fix everything, but you can still choose honesty, forgiveness, and compassion today. And those choices matter more than you think. A word of wisdom, a sincere apology, a final story told with love—these ripple forward into the lives of people who will carry them long after you're gone.

For the Legacy Keeper, ethics isn't about rules anymore, it's about character. The question narrows to something simple: *When people remember me, will they remember someone who made life heavier, or lighter?*

At this stage, responsibility transforms from burden to gift. It's the way you prove, even in your later years, that your life wasn't just lived for yourself, but for the people who came after.

F: Ibrahim Commentary – Ethics: Everyone Loves It Until It Costs Them

Here's the thing about ethics: everybody loves to talk about it, but nobody loves to pay the price for it. We all want to be "good people," but preferably in ways that are convenient, flattering, and Instagrammable.

Being fair when it costs you nothing? Easy. Being honest when lying would save your butt? Suddenly the room gets very quiet.

Hypocrisy is the human default setting. Politicians preach family values while cheating on their spouses. Companies market "sustainability" while pumping out oceans of plastic. Parents tell their kids not to lie, then fake sick days for themselves. And every single one of them justifies it: *I had no choice. It's different in my case. Everybody does it.* Translation: "I like ethics, but I like shortcuts better."

But here's the kicker—ethics isn't about what you say, it's about what you do when it's inconvenient. It's easy to look virtuous when the spotlights on you. The real test is in the moments nobody sees—the promises you keep when you could get away with breaking them, the apologies you give when no one's demanding them, the responsibilities you shoulder even when you're tired and nobody's clapping.

Every stage of life proves this in its own way. At twelve, ethics is about fairness—sharing the candy, telling the truth, owning up when you screw up. At twenty-five, it's about realizing you're not the exception to the rules, even when cutting corners looks tempting. At forty-five, it's about keeping your integrity intact under pressure, when people are watching and depending on you. And at ninety, it's about looking back and asking whether your choices added up to a life worth remembering.

The dirty little secret? Nobody nails this perfectly. We all lie, cheat, flake, and rationalize. The point isn't perfection—it's course correction. Ethics is less about never slipping and more about not letting the slip become the story of your life. Responsibility isn't punishment, it's the proof that you matter, because someone else is counting on you.

So yeah, ethics is messy. It's not black and white, it's a million shades of human compromise. But here's the truth bomb: if you want your life to mean something beyond your own pleasures and achievements, ethics is the currency. It's how you leave people better instead of bitter.

And if you're still not convinced, let us put it this way: nobody wants their eulogy to read, "Well, at least they recycled."

G: Actions – Practicing Ethics & Responsibility

For the 12-Year-Old Explorer
Do one fair thing today. Share your snack, apologize if you messed up, or help with a chore without being asked. Notice how people respond when they realize they can count on you. That's ethics in action.

For the 18–29 Adventurer
Think of one mistake you made recently—big or small. Instead of dodging it, own it. Say the awkward apology. Fix what you can. Responsibility doesn't shrink your dignity—it multiplies it.

For the 30–60 Chaos Survivor
Pick one area where you know you're not living in line with your values—your work, your parenting, your friendships, your health. Take one step this

week to close the gap. It doesn't have to be huge, but it has to be honest.

For the 60–99 Legacy Keeper
Sponsor a cause. Make a donation—of time or money—to a charity or community project you believe in. A legacy isn't just what you tell people; it's what you actively support and empower.

For Everyone: The Seed and the Echo

A walnut seed is small — fragile, almost forgettable. But within its shell, the blueprint for forests sleeps. From that one seed, thousands of trees can rise. And from each of those trees, millions of other seeds can scatter on the wind.

That's not just biology. That's the geometry of influence — the quiet, exponential miracle of life paying forward what it has received.

Your voice is exactly that kind of seed. Your words may drift into silence for years before they take root in someone else's heart. A single sentence you speak today might ripple across generations. The compassion you show a stranger might ignite their courage to do the same for others.

This is the paradox of impact: we rarely witness the forests that grow from our smallest acts. But they grow nonetheless.

And yet, as you plant your seeds — words, kindnesses, ideas — you will encounter the weeds: voices of greed, cruelty, and domination. The world has always produced those who build walls instead of orchards; men and women who treat humanity like property and the Earth like fuel.

Dr. Jane Goodall, near the end of her extraordinary life, spoke of this tension with clarity and grace. She admitted there were people she could never like — those who ruled through fear, silenced compassion, and tore apart ecosystems for their own gain. Yet her message wasn't one of revenge, but of *responsibility.*

From where she said she now "looks down," she asked humanity to remember one truth:

Every one of us has a role to play.
Every one of us matters.
Every day, in small ways, we shape the future we will never see.

She urged us not to surrender to bitterness, but to act — to speak, to plant, to protect.
Because to go silent is to let extinction take root — not just of species, but of spirit.

Evil, after all, thrives not because it is strong, but because goodness grows tired.
It is the silence of the kind, not the noise of the cruel, that allows darkness to spread.

The Garden or the Grave

Hate is the poison ivy of the human heart — seductive, quick to spread, hard to uproot once it wraps itself around your identity.
Greed waters it. Fear fertilizes it.

And soon, the heart forgets how to be soil for anything else.

When a person's need to be *better than* others outweighs their desire to *be better for* others, they begin to rot from the inside out.
When we let our insecurities harden into arrogance, our pain into prejudice, our fear into false superiority — we stop being gardeners of life and become vandals of creation.

To despise another human being because they are female, or LGBTQ, or worship differently, or look different — that is not righteousness; it is rebellion against your own humanity.
You were not born to hate. You were *taught* to.
And anything that can be taught can be *untaught.*

No soul was sent to Earth to dominate, humiliate, or hoard.
You were sent here to learn, to help, to love, and to evolve.
That is the curriculum of existence.

Hate, greed, and judgment are simply ways to drop out of that school early — to forfeit your purpose before your story is even finished.

So when you find yourself tempted to judge or compare, pause and remember:
Every person you see is fighting to bloom in their own way, under their own weather.
Your task is not to pull up their roots — it's to learn how to grow alongside them.

The Light that Outlasts the Shadow

If your kindness feels small, remember: so did the seed that became the forest.

If your courage feels thin, remember: roots grow in silence before they rise toward the sun.

If your hope falters, look to the soil beneath your own feet — it remembers every fallen leaf, every drop of rain, every life that once gave itself to make this ground fertile for you.

You are not here by accident.

You are the continuation of a thousand unspoken promises.

You are both the seed and the echo — what life gives and what life remembers.

So plant deliberately. Speak bravely.

Because even in the darkest climate — moral or physical — hope is not lost.

It is only waiting for someone to scatter it again.

And if you must be anything in this world —

Be the voice that plants understanding, not the noise that harvests hate.

Be the hand that heals the soil, not the one that salts it out of spite.

Be the gardener of grace.

Because that, my friend, is why you are here.

That completes **Chapter 8: Ethics & Responsibility – How to Live Without Being a Jerk.**

Chapter 9: Spiritual & Cosmic Context – Plugging Into Something Bigger

A: Opening Scene – Religion, Seatbelts, and the Human Hunger for Cosmic Context

Humans invented religion the same way they invented seatbelts: to feel safer in a world that will eventually kill us. Fire, floods, disease, earthquakes, you name it, we've faced it. And somewhere along the line, we realized that saying, "There must be a bigger plan" was more comforting than, "Wow, this planet is trying to eat us alive."

From the beginning, we've looked up at the stars and whispered, *What does it all mean?* And because silence is unbearable, we filled it with answers: gods, myths, rituals, sacred texts, constellations that looked suspiciously like farm animals. Whether it was Zeus hurling lightning bolts, Yahweh writing commandments, or modern physicists saying, "It's all quantum fields," the craving is the same—we want to know where we fit in the grand mess.

Even the people who say they don't care, do. The atheist who rolls their eyes at prayer will still feel something stirring when they stand under a night sky scattered with galaxies. The nihilist who insists "nothing matters" still chooses a favorite band, a favorite drink, a person they'd crawl through glass for. Everyone plugs into something bigger, whether they admit it or not.

And in the modern world, the menu of cosmic connection has only expanded. Religion still commands billions, but now we also have science documentaries narrated by Morgan Freeman, psychedelic retreats in the desert, yoga studios with more candles than a fire hazard code should allow, and late-night YouTube rabbit holes that end with Carl Sagan whispering about star stuff. Some people find transcendence in God, others in physics equations, others in staring at their kid's face and realizing, *Oh. That's the miracle.*

But here's the funny part: we keep arguing about whose cosmic context is "right," as if meaning is a zero-sum game. Meanwhile, the real truth is simpler: humans crave something bigger because deep down we know we're small, temporary, and fragile. And admitting that without some bigger frame feels terrifying.

This chapter isn't about telling you which story to believe. It's about exploring the fact that we all need *a* story... a cosmic context, a connection to something larger than ourselves—because without it, existence starts to feel like a bad improv show with no script and no ending.

Whether you call it God, universe, science, spirit, or "the ineffable mystery of why avocados cost so much," the need is the same: we want to belong to something bigger.

B: Spirituality for the 12-Year-Old Explorer

At twelve, spirituality usually shows up as wonder, not theology. It's lying in the grass at night, staring at the stars, and feeling very, very small. It's asking, "Where did Grandma go after she died?" It's wondering why bad things happen, why some kids are bullies, why people pray, or why the sky looks endless.

At this stage, spirituality isn't about certainty, it's about questions. And kids are natural philosophers. They'll ask things adults are too scared to ask: "Why does God let people get sick?" "What happens when you die?" "If the universe goes on forever, what's on the other side?" These questions sound simple, but they're the same one's humanity has been wrestling with since we figured out how to draw on cave walls.

This is also when stories matter most. Kids may not sit through a sermon, but they'll lean forward for myths, parables, and bedtime tales about heroes, gods, and mysteries. Stories give shape to the big questions, even if the answers are symbolic. The myth of the afterlife, the story of creation, even a Pixar movie about souls and emotions—these narratives help a twelve-year-old try to map the unknown.

The danger here is shutting curiosity down too soon. Adults get uncomfortable with the big questions. They hand out easy answers or say, "Don't ask that." But the truth is, spirituality begins with wonder. When kids are allowed to sit in awe—even if the question has no answer—they learn that mystery is part of life.

So at twelve, spirituality isn't about rules or rituals. It's about letting wonder crack you open. It's about noticing the hugeness of the sky, the strangeness of life, the mystery of death—and realizing, even if you can't explain it, that it matters.

Because in the end, those first questions of wonder are the seeds of every adult's spiritual search. And if you can protect that curiosity, you'll never stop seeing the cosmos as the miracle it actually is.

C: Spirituality for the 18–29 Adventurer

Your twenties are where the cosmic questions start to get loud. Maybe you grew up in church, synagogue, mosque, temple, or with no religion at all. Maybe you memorized prayers or maybe your family's idea of "spirituality" was watching Bill Nye reruns. Either way, this is the era when you start deciding what's yours and what's just hand-me-down belief.

For some, this means clinging tighter to tradition. For others, it means walking away entirely. For many, it means wandering—a little faith here, a little doubt there, maybe a weekend retreat in the woods where you tried meditating but mostly thought about snacks. This is the experimentation stage. Spirituality becomes a patchwork quilt of experiences: travel, psychedelics, activism, art, love, heartbreak. You're not just reading about meaning anymore, you're testing it on your own skin.

Suffering hits hard here, too, and it makes the questions sharper. When your relationship falls apart, when money stress keeps you awake, when someone you love dies too soon—you start asking: *Is anyone listening? Does the universe care? Does it mean anything, or is it just chaos?* Doubt feels like failure, but it's not. Doubt is actually part of the spiritual process. Faith without doubt is just autopilot.

The danger in your twenties is nihilism—deciding nothing matters because you don't have all the answers yet. It's tempting to hide behind irony, cynicism, or endless distraction. But nihilism isn't bravery; it's boredom in a trench coat. The real courage is staying open to wonder, even when you're unsure.

Transcendence in your twenties might not look like church pews or prayer rugs. It might be standing at a concert with your best friends, feeling the bass rattle your bones. It might be hiking up a mountain and realizing you're tiny against the skyline. It might be holding someone you love and thinking, *This is it. This is the point.*

At this stage, spirituality isn't about certainty, it's about exploration. You're building your own language for awe. You're testing your compass. You're learning that cosmic context doesn't always give answers, but it always gives perspective. And perspective is what makes the chaos survivable.

D: Spirituality for the 30–60 Chaos Survivor

By the time you've traded all-nighters at the bar for all-nighters with a sick kid or a looming deadline, the big cosmic questions don't go away, they just get buried under soccer practices, deadlines, tax forms, and late-night Amazon orders you regret in the morning. You don't stop wondering about the meaning of life—you just forget you were wondering until grief, crisis, or silence knocks you back into it.

This is the age when spirituality often shifts from theory to necessity. In your twenties, you could debate faith over drinks at 2 a.m. By your forties, you're whispering prayers in hospital waiting rooms or staring at the ceiling at 3 a.m. wondering if the job that's draining you to death is really what life was supposed to be about. You don't need abstract answers, you need something steady to hold onto when the ground keeps moving.

For some, that's religion. For others, it's meditation, therapy, or walking into the woods until the noise dies down. Some people return to the faith they left years ago. Others double down on science, philosophy, or pure awe at the universe. Some just find transcendence in rituals, family dinners, community service, weekly hikes, lighting a candle. Whatever the form, the hunger is the same: *Give me something bigger than this grind.*

The danger here is spiritual autopilot. You get so used to the chaos that you stop asking questions at all. You numb yourself with work, with screens, with substances, with sheer busyness. You convince yourself you don't have time for awe. But without that connection, life shrinks down to nothing but tasks and transactions.

Spirituality at this stage doesn't need to be dramatic. It's often about small, steady practices—ten minutes of silence, gratitude before bed, looking at the stars instead of your phone. It's about remembering you're not the center of the universe, but you're also not alone in it.

Because when the weight gets heavy—and it will—the only thing that lightens it is remembering that you are part of something larger! That your pain isn't wasted, your love isn't meaningless, your existence isn't just a cosmic accident. Whether you call that God, the universe, or simply wonder, the point is the same: you're not just grinding. You're connected.

E: Spirituality for the 60–99 Legacy Keeper

By the time you reach your sixties, seventies, eighties, and beyond, the cosmic questions aren't background noise anymore—they're front and center. You've buried people you love. Your body is slowing down. The horizon looks closer than it used to. And whether you were a churchgoer, a skeptic, or somewhere in between, the question presses: *What comes next?*

For some, this is a return to faith. Old prayers come back like muscle memory. Rituals that once felt routine now glow with depth. Others lean into philosophy, into nature, into storytelling. Some find comfort in the science of stardust—remembering that when we die, we return to the cosmos that made us. Others find it in scripture, in hymns, in sacred stories they now see with fresh eyes.

113

Spirituality at this stage often blends awe with acceptance. The universe is vast. Life is brief. But brevity doesn't erase meaning—it intensifies it. The sunset is more beautiful when you know you won't see infinite more. A laugh with your grandchildren is sweeter because you know time is short. Mortality sharpens joy like nothing else can.

Suffering is heavier here—loss of friends, health, independence. But transcendence isn't magic; it's a perspective shift. It's the moment you finally release a grudge that's been living rent-free in your head for forty years. It's the choice to find beauty in the cracks instead of just seeing what's broken. It's choosing, even now, to be a student of wonder, not a prisoner of memory. Spirituality here isn't about conquering death—it's about making peace with it and leaving something luminous behind.

And here's the most powerful truth: you don't have to know the answers. Maybe you believe in heaven. Maybe you believe in reincarnation. Maybe you believe in nothing but atoms returning to the stars. What matters is that you lived like it meant something—that your presence touched others, that your stories continue, that your love outlives you.

At this stage, spirituality stops being about proof. It becomes about presence. About belonging to the great story, however you name it, and trusting that your small chapter mattered.

F: Ibrahim Commentary – God, Cosmos, and the Great Human Shrug

Here's the cosmic joke: everyone thinks they've got it figured out. The devout believer says, "I know exactly what happens when we die." The hardcore atheist says, "I know exactly what *doesn't* happen when we die." Both are suspiciously confident about a mystery nobody's ever come back to file a Yelp review on. You can be devout or a non-believer, that doesn't matter. What does is that you need to acknowledge that we are all connected somehow.

Meanwhile, the rest of us are standing in the middle, staring up at the stars, going: *This is huge, I am small, and I really hope I'm not screwing this up.*

Dogmatists annoy us because they treat mystery like a solved math problem. "Here are the rules, follow them, and you'll get the cosmic prize." Nihilists annoy us because they act like shrugging is enlightenment. "Nothing matters, so why bother?" Congrats, you've reinvented apathy. Neither extreme does justice to the actual human experience: awe, confusion, longing, wonder, and the desperate need to make sense of it all.

Spirituality isn't about answers about connection. It's not about having the right doctrine or the right TED Talk. It's about plugging into the bigger picture, whatever name you give it: God, the universe, nature, consciousness, love, science, stardust. Call it what you want. The important part is realizing you're not the center of the story, but you're also not irrelevant. You're a thread in a much larger tapestry.

Every stage of life proves this. At twelve, spirituality is raw wonder—why is the sky so big? Where do pets go when they die? At twenty-five, it's wrestling with belief and doubt, trying new languages for awe. At forty-five, it's searching for stability in the middle of chaos, clinging to small rituals that connect you to the bigger picture. And at ninety, it's acceptance— knowing you'll never have all the answers, but that your chapter still matters.

The real tragedy isn't that we don't know the cosmic truth. It's that we waste our lives either pretending we do or pretending it doesn't matter. The win is staying awake to mystery. Standing in the middle of the mess, the beauty, the suffering, and still whispering, *Wow.*

So no, you don't need to have the universe figured out. You just need to stay connected—to wonder, to others, to the story that's bigger than you. That's spirituality. That's cosmic context. That's the seatbelt we invented to remind ourselves that the ride is worth taking.

G: Actions – Practicing Spirituality & Cosmic Context

For the 12-Year-Old Explorer
Next time you see something that makes you go "whoa"—a sunset, a weird bug, the stars—don't rush past it. Stop. Stare. Ask one big question about it. "Why is the sky orange?" "Where did that star come from?" That question is the start of your spiritual compass.

For the 18–29 Adventurer
Try one new practice of awe this week. It could be meditation, prayer, journaling, stargazing,

volunteering, even sitting in silence for ten minutes without your phone. Notice what cracks you open, what makes you feel connected instead of distracted.

For the 30–60 Chaos Survivor
Schedule ten minutes a week for big-picture mode. Walk outside, read something that stirs your soul, pray, or just look at the night sky instead of your inbox. It's not wasted time—it's the anchor that keeps you from drowning in busyness.

For the 60–99 Legacy Keeper
Create a place of wonder. This could be a small garden, a bird feeder outside your window, or a bookshelf filled with books that expanded your mind. Create a physical space that invites others to pause and connect with something bigger.

That completes **Chapter 9: Spiritual & Cosmic Context – Plugging Into Something Bigger.**

Chapter 10: Mortality & Legacy – The Final Exam

A: Opening Scene – Death, Undefeated Champion of Existence

Death is undefeated. It doesn't matter how rich you are, how many green smoothies you drink, or how many CrossFit burpees you survive, nobody gets out alive. Somewhere, the Grim Reaper is laughing his bony ass off, because every human being who's ever walked this planet has ended up in the same place: gone.

And yet, we act like it's optional. We Botox, we bio hack, we chase eternal youth like it's a limited-time coupon code. Tech billionaires are pouring fortunes into immortality projects, like death is just a bug in the system waiting for a software patch. Hate to break it to them: death isn't a glitch, it's the operating system.

Our culture hides from it. We tuck death away in hospitals, funeral homes, and polite silences. We binge-watch shows where a hundred people get murdered per season but ask us to talk about real grief and suddenly the room gets quieter than the library at midnight. We avoid writing wills, we skip hard conversations, we treat aging like a disease instead of the price of existing. We're obsessed with youth, because youth let us keep pretending, we've got forever.

But here's the paradox: mortality is the very thing that gives life meaning. If you had endless time, nothing would matter. Deadlines wouldn't exist. Urgency would disappear. The beauty of a sunset would fade if you knew you had infinite more coming. Love wouldn't feel so desperate or precious if you knew you could fall into it a thousand times without consequence. Death is the timer that makes the game worth playing.

And legacy? That's our loophole. If death says, "Your time is limited," legacy answers, "Maybe so, but pieces of me can live on." Legacy isn't just monuments or biographies. It's the impact you have, the laughter you left in a friend's memory, the stories you told, the lessons you passed down, the love that shaped your family. Legacy is how humans cheat death—not by dodging it, but by refusing to be erased completely.

So no, death is not the enemy. It's the final exam. And how you live now—the stories you create, the people you touch, the ripples you send forward—is how you prepare for it. That's what this chapter is about: facing the undefeated champion, not with denial, but with clarity.

Because once you accept that your time is short, the question sharpens to something urgent and beautiful: *What will you do with the time you have?*

B: Mortality for the 12-Year-Old Explorer

119

At twelve, mortality usually comes crashing in for the first time. Maybe it's the death of a grandparent, a neighbor, a classmate's parent. Maybe it's your first pet—gone overnight, leaving you staring at an empty food bowl like it's some cruel magic trick. At that age, death feels unfair, confusing, too big for your brain to wrap around.

Adults try to soften the blow. "Grandmas in a better place." "Your dog crossed the rainbow bridge." "He's sleeping forever." Which, let's be honest, is terrifying if you're a kid who now thinks sleeping is a gateway drug to the afterlife. The metaphors are meant to help, but what they really reveal is how awkward adults are at talking about death.

For a twelve-year-old, mortality often sparks the first real cosmic question: *Where do people go? Why do they leave? Will it happen to me?* It's a terrifying thought—realizing that life doesn't stretch on forever. That one day, everyone you know will be gone, and so will you. It's like suddenly being told the rules of a game you didn't know you were playing.

But alongside the fear comes the first lessons in legacy. You learn that people live on in memories, stories, pictures, and the ways they shaped your life. Maybe you repeat a joke your grandfather told you, or you still draw the way your mom taught you, or you plant flowers because your neighbor always loved them. Suddenly, you realize: gone doesn't mean erased.

This is also the age where kids begin to wonder how they'll be remembered. Not in big, dramatic terms, but in little ways. Will their friends remember them as funny? Kind? The kid who always shared their snacks. Legacy starts small at twelve—it's how your presence lingers in the people around you.

Mortality at this stage feels unfair. Legacy feels abstract. But both plant seeds. You're beginning to understand that life isn't endless, and that meaning is found in how you shape the small piece of it you're given. And even if you don't have all the words for it yet, you're learning that the way you live leaves echoes behind.

C: Mortality for the 18–29 Adventurer

In your twenties, mortality shows up like an uninvited guest at a party you thought would last forever. Up until now, death felt like something that happened to old people, or in movies, or to someone else far away. But then it happens closer. A friend in a car accident. A relative gone too soon. A headline that shakes you because the victim is your age. Suddenly, immortality feels like the scam it always was.

This is the stage where you first realize: *I'm not untouchable.* And it hits hard. You start thinking differently when you drive too fast, when you drink too much, when you see someone your age buried. Mortality stops being a word and starts being a possibility. It feels unfair. It feels terrifying. But it also wakes you up.

Legacy begins to take root here too—not in grand gestures, but in the ripples you start leaving behind.

121

The friendships you build. The love you give (or take for granted). The art you make, the work you do, the causes you fight for, even the memes you create that get passed around long after you've stopped caring about them. Your twenties are the first time you realize your life is shaping a footprint, whether you mean to or not.

The danger here is overcorrecting. Some people spiral into nihilism—*we all die, so nothing matters.* Others swing the opposite way, chasing "bucket list" highs and acting like legacy has to mean changing the world before thirty. But here's the truth: legacy doesn't have to be loud. It's not about scale—it's about impact. The way you show up for people today is the beginning of how you'll be remembered tomorrow.

Death in your twenties is a harsh teacher, but it sharpens perspective. Suddenly the fights you had with friends feel stupid. The little stresses at work feel smaller. What matters grows clearer: connection, love, laughter, contribution. That clarity—painful as it is—is mortality's first gift.

So yes, your twenties should be full of exploration and freedom. But don't ignore mortality when it taps you on the shoulder. It's not there to ruin the party. It's there to remind you: this is your one wild, fragile shot. Don't waste it.

D: Mortality for the 30–60 Chaos Survivor

By your thirties, forties, and fifties, death has lost its shock value. It's not just something that happens "out there." It's here. Parents pass. Friends are diagnosed. Coworkers collapse at their desks. The obituary section starts to include people you actually knew. The invincibility of your twenties is long gone, replaced by a quiet awareness: *we don't have forever.*

This is also when your own body begins filing complaints. The late nights that used to feel like nothing now take three days to recover from. Knees ache. Backs protest. The doctor starts using words like "cholesterol," "risk factor," and "we should keep an eye on that." Mortality stops being theory, it's in the mirror.

And this awareness shifts how you think about legacy. Suddenly, it's not just a vague "someday" idea. It's your kids, if you have them. It's your work, your art, your leadership, your friendships, your impact on the people around you. You start asking: *Am I building something that will outlast me, or just grinding in circles until I disappear?*

The danger here is denial. You get so busy carrying responsibilities—raising kids, paying mortgages, climbing career ladders—that you forget life is short. You tell yourself you'll write the book, start the project, repair the relationship "later." But "later" is a lie mortality doesn't honor. Eventually, the bill comes due.

The flip side is motivation. Mortality can light a fire. It pushes you to be intentional: to stop wasting years on jobs that drain you, to say the things you've been holding back, to prioritize people over prestige. Death isn't pleasant to think about, but it's the best clarity machine you'll ever have.

Legacy at this stage isn't abstract daily. It's in how you raise your kids, how you mentor younger coworkers, how you treat your partner when you're tired, how you contribute to your community. It's not the "big" things that define you—it's the accumulation of choices. Someday, those choices will be the stories people tell when you're gone.

So if you're in this stretch of life, here's the hard but liberating truth: you don't have endless time. Which means the time you *do* have is wildly precious. And every choice—how you spend your hours, how you treat people, what you build—is already shaping the legacy you'll leave.

E: Mortality for the 60–99 Legacy Keeper

By the time you reach your sixties, seventies, eighties, and beyond, mortality is no longer theoretical... it's right there at the table with you. You feel it in your body, in the empty chairs where friends used to sit, in the quiet of mornings that once held more noise. You don't have to imagine death; you've lived through enough of it to know it's real, and it's coming for you, too.

This awareness changes everything. Suddenly, time isn't abstract—it's finite, countable. Every season feels sharper, every birthday heavier, every laugh more precious. Mortality becomes less about fear and more about focus: *What do I do with what's left?*

And the answer is legacy. Not legacy in the Hollywood sense—not fame, statues, or buildings named after you. Legacy here is simpler, deeper. It's the stories you've told. The lessons you've passed down. The love you've given, the forgiveness you've offered, the wisdom you've shared. Legacy is the ripple you leave in other people's lives.

At this stage, you start seeing legacy in action. A grandchild repeats your joke. A former student quotes your advice. A community still remembers your service. Your fingerprints are all over lives that continue after you. And that realization—*I mattered*—is a form of transcendence.

But there's also regret. The calls not made. The forgiveness not offered. The risks never taken. The danger at this stage is letting regret define your legacy instead of reshaping it. And here's the good news: it's not too late. Legacy is alive until your last breath. One conversation, one letter, one story can still ripple forward.

Spiritual traditions often frame this stage as preparation—setting your affairs in order, reconciling, reflecting, passing wisdom on. Mortality demands honesty: no more illusions of forever, just the truth of now. And in that honesty, life takes on a kind of clarity and beauty that the young rarely see.

At sixty, seventy, ninety—you don't need to chase immortality. You're already immortal in the people you've touched. That's the gift of legacy: proof that even when your story ends, your echoes continue.

**F: Ken Commentary – Death Isn't Optional,
Legacy Is**

Here's a fun fact about your body: you're just
renting. And death is the landlord who never loses
an eviction notice. It doesn't matter how well you've
maintained the property or how many
'improvements' you've made, the lease has an
expiration date, and it's non-negotiable. Still, we
spend our lives trying to argue the terms, dumping
billions into life-extension like we're trying to buy
the building. We Botox the cracks, biohack the
plumbing, and pretend we can just squat here
forever. Hate to break it to you, but you can't. The
only question is what you do with the place before
you have to hand over the keys.

The problem isn't dying—it's our refusal to face it.
We treat death like Voldemort: "He Who Must Not Be
Named." We sanitize funerals, whisper about cancer,
avoid writing wills, and act like "later" is a
guaranteed setting on the calendar. Meanwhile,
death is standing in the corner, sipping a latte,
waiting for us to stop being ridiculous.

Here's the kicker: mortality is not the enemy. It's the
clarity machine. If you had forever, nothing would
matter. Deadlines wouldn't exist. Risks would be
optional. Love would feel disposable. Death is what
sharpens everything. It's the timer that makes the
game worth playing.

And legacy? That's the loophole. Death may claim
your body, but it can't erase the ripples you leave
behind—unless you never bothered to make any.
Legacy isn't fame, fortune, or some monument with

your name on it. It's the kid who remembers your kindness, the friend who repeats your advice, the student who builds on what you taught them. Legacy is living proof that you mattered.

Every stage of life wrestles with this truth. At twelve, death feels unfair, and legacy shows up in memories of pets and grandparents. At twenty-five, death shocks you with its closeness, and legacy feels like the impact you're just starting to make. At forty-five, mortality is the gut-check that makes you ask, "Am I living on purpose or just grinding in circles?" And at ninety, death is reality, but legacy is the comfort—you see your fingerprints in the lives still unfolding around you.

So here's the hard but freeing truth: you don't get to skip death. But you do get to choose your legacy. Every day, with every choice, you're writing the stories people will tell when you're gone. And if that thought scares you—good. It means you're paying attention.

Death isn't optional. Legacy is. And the sooner you face that, the sooner you stop wasting your one wild shot pretending you've got forever.

G: Actions – Practicing Mortality & Legacy

For the 12-Year-Old Explorer
Think of someone you miss—a pet, a grandparent, a friend who moved away. Share one memory about them with someone else. That's how legacy works: telling stories so people live on in echoes.

For the 18–29 Adventurer

Write one sentence of your "living eulogy." What would you want people to say about you at your funeral—not in some grand, perfect way, but in a simple truth? Use that as a compass for how you're showing up today.

For the 30–60 Chaos Survivor

Choose one legacy action this week. Teach someone a skill, repair a broken relationship, mentor a younger coworker, write a letter to someone who matters. Don't wait for "someday"—someday is a myth death doesn't recognize.

For the 60–99 Legacy Keeper

Write your "ethical will." This isn't about your possessions; it's a letter to your loved ones sharing your values, your hopes for their future, and the love you have for them. It's a final, intentional piece of your heart left behind.

That completes **Chapter 10: Mortality & Legacy – The Final Exam.**

Chapter 11: So What Now? – Living the Meaning Day by Day

A: Opening Scene – Congrats, You Read a Book on the Meaning of Life. Now What?

Congratulations, you've just read a book about the meaning of life. Do you get a certificate now? A decoder ring? Maybe a secret password that unlocks enlightenment? Sorry to disappoint—no badges, no Jedi robes, no enlightenment points you can cash in for free smoothies. All you've got is... Tuesday.

That's the trick nobody tells you. You can read a hundred books, binge every TED Talk, meditate on a mountaintop, or even argue with philosophers in a smoky café—and at the end of it, you'll still wake up tomorrow to emails, dishes, laundry, kids, bills, and that weird rattle your car is making. Life doesn't pause for your epiphanies.

Which is why meaning can't just live in theories and big cosmic questions. Meaning has to fit inside the ordinary. Otherwise, it's useless. If your "purpose" only works on a spiritual retreat or after your third ayahuasca trip, it's not purpose—it's a vacation. Real meaning has to survive Tuesday mornings, Monday deadlines, and Friday traffic jams.

The good news is, you don't need some huge revelation to start living meaningfully. You already have the tools—awareness, connection, growth, contribution, joy, endurance, responsibility, wonder, legacy. They're all sitting in your pocket, waiting to be used. The problem isn't that you don't know enough—it's that you don't practice what you already know.

So this chapter is about the "so what?" It's about shrinking all those big truths into small, doable moves you can actually carry into your messy, beautiful, stressful, ordinary days. Because meaning isn't discovered once—it's practiced daily.

No gold star required.

B: The Daily Meaning Practice – Nine Simple Moves

Forget the 47-step morning routines you see on Instagram. You don't need to drink yak butter tea at sunrise or journal in gold-leaf notebooks while balancing on a Himalayan rock. Meaning isn't built in rituals you'll abandon in three days—it's built in simple, repeatable moves that you can sneak into an ordinary Tuesday.

Here are nine meaning moves—each tied to the core understandings we've explored. Do them daily if you can, but even catching one or two keeps you on track. Think of them as reps for your humanity.

1. Notice (Awareness)
Spend one minute noticing that you exist. Sounds dumb, right? But sit still, breathe, and go: *I'm here.*

I'm alive. This is my body. This is my day. That pause is the mirror of consciousness—and it sharpens every other part of life.

2. Connect (Belonging)
Send one text, make one call, or say one kind word to someone you care about. That's it. Connection doesn't require group therapy or family reunions. It's the micro-moments—"thinking of you," "thanks for that," "I love you"—that glue life together.

3. Grow (Learning)
Learn one new thing daily. It can be tiny. A word, a fact, a skill, a correction. Growth doesn't always feel dramatic, but it keeps you from becoming stale wallpaper.

4. Contribute (Purpose)
Do one thing that makes life better for someone else. Hold the door, share your knowledge, fix the damn printer. Purpose doesn't always look like grand speeches—it often looks like leaving a room (or Zoom) better than you found it.

5. Savor (Joy)
Pause once a day to enjoy something just because it exists—your coffee, your kid's laugh, that song you can't stop replaying. Joy isn't extra credit—it's the fuel that makes the grind survivable.

6. Endure (Suffering)
When pain hits (and it will), don't just numb it. Name it. Say, "This hurts." Then breathe through it. Endurance isn't denial—it's allowing pain to exist without letting it own you.

7. Choose (Ethics)

Make one conscious choice today that aligns with your values—even when it's inconvenient. Tell the truth. Keep the promise. Say no to something you shouldn't say yes to. Responsibility is practiced in the smallest decisions.

8. Wonder (Spirituality)

Once a day, look up—literally or metaphorically. Stare at the sky, listen to a song that wrecks you, read something that cracks your brain open. Wonder keeps you connected to the bigger story.

9. Remember (Mortality & Legacy)

Before bed, ask: *If today were my last, what would I want to be remembered for?* No panic—just perspective. Legacy is built one day at a time.

You don't have to nail all nine every day. This isn't cosmic bingo. But if you touch even a few, you'll feel the thread running through your life. Not as a theory, but as a rhythm.

Because meaning isn't a revelation. It's a practice.

C: Ken Commentary – Why You'll Fail at This (and Why That's Fine)

Let's be clear: you're going to fail at this. Not once, not twice, but constantly. You'll forget to notice. You'll ignore texts. You'll binge Netflix instead of learning something new. You'll lie to yourself, flake on someone, eat like a raccoon in a dumpster, and then beat yourself up because you're not living like the Dalai Lama with a productivity app.

Good. That's called being alive.

The problem with most "meaning of life" advice is that it's written as if you're a robot who can flawlessly execute the same perfect routine every day. Wake up at 5 a.m., hydrate with imported mineral water, meditate for an hour, journal your intentions, run ten miles, solve world hunger, all before breakfast. Meanwhile, the rest of us are trying to find matching socks. Reality check: you're going to sleep in, spill coffee on yourself, and doomscroll before bed. Congratulations, you're human.

Here's the truth nobody tells you: meaning isn't about consistency, it's about course correction. You don't lose the thread when you miss a day. You lose it when you decide the thread doesn't matter anymore.

Think about it. If you forget to call a friend one day, you can still call tomorrow. If you blow up at your kid, you can still apologize. If you numb out with ice cream instead of facing your feelings, you can still face them next time. The thread doesn't unravel because of one knot. Meaning is resilient—as long as you keep showing up, it keeps weaving.

So, stop aiming for perfection. Forget cosmic bingo. Forget influencer routines. Forget trying to live like every day is an Instagram highlight reel. Living meaningfully is about small, repeated, imperfect acts. It's messy, it's uneven, it's full of failures—but those failures are part of the tapestry. They give it texture.

So yes, you will fail at this. Again and again. And every time you pick the thread back up, you're proving that your life still has meaning. Not because it's flawless, but because it's lived.

D: Actions – Daily Integration for Every Age Door

For the 12-Year-Old Explorer
Each day, pick one "meaning move." Maybe you share your snack (connection), notice the sky (wonder), or learn one new fact (growth). Write it down or tell someone about it before bed. You'll start to see your life as a story you're already shaping.

For the 18–29 Adventurer
Build a five-minute ritual. It could be journaling, walking without your phone, praying, or sending a check-in text to a friend. The ritual isn't about grand meaning—it's about anchoring your chaotic days with one moment of intention.

For the 30–60 Chaos Survivor
Each night, ask yourself one question: *What actually mattered today?* Write down one answer. That's it. Over time, you'll build a ledger of what truly counts, and it won't be the emails or errands. It'll be the people, the choices, the sparks of joy.

For the 60–99 Legacy Keeper
Schedule a "legacy date." Once a week, intentionally connect with a younger person—a grandchild, a neighbor, a mentee—and simply be present with them. Ask them about *their* life. Your greatest legacy can be the gift of your focused, loving attention.

That completes **Chapter 11: So What Now? – Living the Meaning Day by Day.**

Chapter 12 : Conclusion

The Thread That Makes You Human Enough

So, did we figure it out? Do you finally know the meaning of life? Good. Write it on a sticky note, slap it on your fridge, and admire your new enlightenment every time you grab a soda. That's it—book over. You're welcome.

Except... you and I both know that's not how this works.

If life were a syllabus, nobody would pass. The assignments would be vague, the grading scale would change every week, and the professor would never answer emails. You'd show up on exam day to discover that half the questions weren't even covered in class. Congratulations: you're flunking existence.

And here's the kicker—you're supposed to.

What we *did* figure out is that life's meaning isn't hiding in some locked chest waiting for you to dig it up like buried treasure. It's a thread. And you've been weaving it the whole time.

So where does that leave us? With the threads you've been weaving all along, the ones that create the messy, imperfect, one-of-a-kind pattern of your life. Let's look at them one last time:

- **Survival & Continuity – The Root**
  Breathing, eating, staying alive. It's the raw foundation—the soil from which everything else grows. Without it, there is no story.

- **Consciousness & Awareness – The Mirror**
  The "I am" that separates you from a goldfish. It's the mirror that lets you reflect, question, and turn mere existence into experience.

- **Connection & Belonging – The Glue** Love, trust, and shared stories. The proof that we are pack animals who thrive not in isolation, but in the warmth of a shared fire.

- **Growth & Learning – The Climb** The slow, uneven climb toward becoming more than you were yesterday, fueled by curiosity, mistakes, and breakthroughs.

- **Purpose & Contribution – The Imprint** The fingerprint you leave on the world, proving you mattered beyond your own survival.

- **Joy & Experience – The Spark** Laughter, beauty, awe. The sparks that remind you that being alive is worth the struggle.

- **Suffering & Transcendence – The Forge**
  The universal pain that can either harden you into stone or forge you into something deeper, stronger, and more compassionate.

- **Ethics & Responsibility – The Compass**
  The guide that prevents your story from becoming someone else's cautionary tale.

- **Spiritual & Cosmic Context – The Horizon**
  The sense that you're part of a larger story, whether you find it in God, science, nature, or wonder.

- **Mortality & Legacy – The Timer** The ticking clock that makes life urgent, and the echo you leave behind that makes it meaningful.

When you weave them together, you don't get perfection. You get *you*. The mistake people make is thinking they'll find meaning all at once, like a grand finale. No—meaning sneaks up on you. It's in the phone call you made, the apology you gave, the joke that made someone's day. Meaning isn't the destination; it's the texture of the road. And the good news is, you don't have to be flawless at walking it.

You just have to be *human enough.*

Ibrahim Commentary – Why You Don't Need to Be Superhuman

Let's get one thing straight: you don't need to be superhuman. You don't need to meditate for three hours a day, run ultra-marathons, drink kale smoothies blessed by Himalayan monks, or optimize your life until you're basically a productivity robot in yoga pants. That's not enlightenment—that's burnout in a fancier costume.

The self-improvement industry makes billions selling you the illusion that you're not enough. That you need *one more habit, one more course, one more hack* before you finally matter. Newsflash: you already matter. You mattered when you screwed up. You mattered when you laughed so hard you snorted.

You mattered when you held someone's hand, or told the truth when it hurt, or just showed up when you didn't want to.

Perfection isn't the goal here. In fact, perfection would ruin the whole thing. Imagine if everyone lived flawlessly—no mistakes, no failures, no regrets. It would be sterile, boring, robotic. A world of saints would be a world without stories. It's the messiness—the cracked edges, the apologies, the laughter through tears, the getting it wrong and trying again—that makes us human. And that humanity is the whole point.

So stop chasing superhuman. Stop thinking meaning is about becoming some idealized, saintly version of yourself. Meaning isn't in flawless routines or shiny achievements. It's in showing up messy, trying again, and letting your life weave together into something real, tangled, and true.

The truth is, you don't need to be more. You don't need to be less. You don't need to be different. You just need to be *human enough*.

That's the punchline of this entire book. Not "perfect enough." Not "holy enough." Not "successful enough." Just human enough. That's where the meaning lives.

Final Actions – Being Human Enough

- **For the 12-Year-Old Explorer:** Your questions are not annoying. They're gold. Keep asking them, even when adults roll their eyes. And keep being kind, even in small ways. That's already meaning.

139

- **For the 18–29 Adventurer:** Relax. Nobody in your age group has it all figured out, no matter what their Instagram says. Pick one thread—joy, growth, connection—and follow it today. That's enough.

- **For the 30–60 Chaos Survivor:** Stop pretending you're failing just because life feels heavy. You're holding multiple threads at once—responsibility, love, struggle, purpose. That's not failure; that's mastery in disguise. Look for the meaning you're already making.

- **For the 60–99 Legacy Keeper:** Your stories are treasure. Tell them, record them, write them down. They don't have to be perfect—they just have to be yours. That's how your thread keeps weaving long after you're gone.

Closing Beat

So here we are. You read the book, you wrestled with the big questions, you got roasted a little, and you probably laughed at least once (if not, that's on us). Did we solve the meaning of life? No. And thank God—or the universe, or the void—that we didn't. Because if we nailed it down to one sentence, the game would be over.

Instead, what you've got is a map, a thread, and a practice. You've got proof that being human—messy, fragile, joyful, resilient, questioning, failing, trying again—is not a flaw in the system. It *is* the system.

You don't need to be superhuman. You don't need to be perfect. You don't need to have all the answers.

You just need to be human enough.

That's the meaning of life. That's the whole thing.

Now close this book. Look around. The search is over. The living is now.

The dishes are waiting.

Epilogue

Frequently Asked Questions About Existence (Ken & Ibrahim Answer Badly but Honestly)

Q: What is the meaning of life, really?
A: Didn't you read the book? Fine, here's the cheat sheet: breathe, love, screw up, laugh, endure, wonder, connect, and leave something behind. That's it. If you want more detail, reread Chapters 1–12. If you want less detail, here's the tweet version: *Don't be a jerk, and remember you're stardust.*

Q: What happens when we die?
A: Honestly? Nobody knows. Anyone who claims certainty is either selling you a religion, a philosophy course, or a podcast. What we *do* know is that your atoms go back into circulation, and your legacy sticks around in the people you've touched. Whether that's reincarnation, heaven, or cosmic recycling— it's above my pay grade.

Q: Why is there so much suffering in the world?
A: Because life is unfair, random, and occasionally cruel. But also because suffering is part of the package. It breaks us, but it also shapes us. The trick isn't avoiding pain—it's learning to forge

meaning out of it without turning bitter. And yes, that's hard. Welcome to the club.

Q: How do I know if I'm living a meaningful life?
A: Do people smile when you walk into a room—or at least not groan? Do you love someone, even imperfectly? Do you keep trying after you screw up? Congrats, you're doing it.

Q: What if I feel like I'm failing at life?
A: You are. We all are. That's literally the definition of life—nobody does it flawlessly. The point isn't to ace it, it's to keep weaving the thread. You'll never feel "finished," but that's not failure—that's being human.

Q: Isn't this all just pointless in the grand scheme of the universe?
A: Sure. If you zoom out far enough, everything is dust and heat death. But meaning doesn't live at the cosmic scale—it lives at the human scale. The universe doesn't care if you laughed today. But the person you laughed with does. That's enough.

Q: Okay, last one—what's the secret?
A: The secret is there is no secret. You don't need a guru, a hack, or a course. You just need to live your life—messy, imperfect, tangled, hilarious, heartbreaking, beautiful. You need to be human enough. That's it. That's the whole damn secret.

Mic drop. Book over. Now go live.

About the Authors

Ken Konet, M.Ed., MBA
Ken Konet is an Instructional Designer, IT Engineer, and HR professional who has spent decades helping people learn, lead, and laugh their way through the messiness of being human. With two MBAs and a master's in education, and quite some time spent at Oxford University in England, Ken blends analytical precision with storytelling warmth. Known for his "Ken Mode"— a mix of Deadpool sarcasm, compassionate mentorship, and philosophical clarity—he writes to make big questions feel personal and possible. His work reminds readers that meaning isn't found in perfection; it's built through practice, purpose, and presence, one imperfect day at a time.

Ibrahim Roble
Ibrahim Roble is a Kenyan systems thinker, educator, and creative philosopher whose work bridges faith, technology, and the human condition. Trained in both science and theology, he explores how reason and spirituality can coexist without contradiction. His voice brings balance to modern existential questions, grounding them in compassion, humility, and curiosity. In *The Meaning of YOUR Life*, Ibrahim helps readers reconnect logic with love, clarity with courage, and purpose with everyday practice.